FRIENDSHIP

GARLAND BIBLIOGRAPHIES IN SOCIOLOGY
General Editor: Dan A. Chekki
(Vol. 4)

GARLAND REFERENCE LIBRARY
OF SOCIAL SCIENCE
(Vol. 244)

GARLAND BIBLIOGRAPHIES IN SOCIOLOGY

General Editor: Dan A. Chekki

1. *Conflict and Conflict Resolution: A Historical Bibliography*
   by Jack Nusan Porter

2. *Sociology of Sciences: An Annotated Bibliography of Invisible Colleges, 1972–1981*
   by Daryl E. Chubin

3. *Race and Ethnic Relations: An Annotated Bibliography*
   by Graham C. Kinloch

4. *Friendship: A Selected, Annotated Bibliography*
   by J.L. Barkas

FRIENDSHIP
A Selected, Annotated Bibliography

Yager, Jan

J.L. Barkas

BJ
1533
F8
Y3145
1985

LAMAR UNIVERSITY LIBRARY

GARLAND PUBLISHING, INC. • NEW YORK & LONDON
1985

© 1985 J.L. Barkas
All rights reserved

Library of Congress Cataloging in Publication Data
Barkas, J. L. (Janet L.)
 Friendship: a bibliography.

 (Garland bibliographies in sociology ; vol. 4)
(Garland reference library of social science ; vol. 244)
 Includes indexes.
 1. Friendship—Bibliography. I. Title. II. Series:
Garland bibliographies in sociology ; v. 4. III. Series:
Garland reference library of social science ; v. 244.
 Z5873.B26 1985 [BJ1533.F8] 016.302 84-48381
 ISBN 0-8240-8937-5 (alk. paper)

Printed on acid-free, 250-year-life paper
Manufactured in the United States of America

For my parents

CONTENTS

Preface of the General Editor	ix
Introduction	xi
Books, Booklets, Dissertations, and Reports	1
Articles (and Chapters) in Journals, Books, Encyclopedias, Magazines, and Newspapers	49
Unpublished Materials: Conferences, Correspondence, Papers, Reports, and Audio-Visuals	103
Organizational Resources	114
Author (and Editor) Index	121
Subject Index	129

PREFACE OF THE GENERAL EDITOR

From Aristotle to Simmel many social thinkers have reflected upon the nature and significance of friendship. Indeed it is difficult to imagine our life without friends. In recent decades our society has been changing rapidly. The complexity, anonymity, impersonality, loneliness and alienation characteristic of urban industrial societies today are said to be non-conducive to the development of a friendship relationship. However, increasing bureaucratization and the rising incidence of singleness and divorce seem to underscore the need for friends as a source of information, empathy and emotional support.

Viewed as a dyadic relationship and as a network, friendship as a type of *gemeinschaft* is a basic social need from childhood to the final years of life. Friendship as a voluntary caring relationship between two or more persons having no kinship or legal bonds tends to reinforce our self-esteem and a feeling of being liked and needed. Although friendship may be categorized by the level of intimacy of the relationship, friends usually share common interests, feelings, experiences and memories.

Most of us may wish to develop skills in making and sustaining friendships at different times in our life. We would like to know how friendship affects our health and intellect. What are the patterns and problems of friendship at various stages of life? What about gender differences in friendship? How to make new friends and how to keep old friends? These and many more significant questions of this nature have been addressed by researchers.

This volume reflects the resurgence of interest, in recent years, in the study of friendship. This emerging area is useful for an adequate understanding of marriage and the family, socialization and sex roles, life cycle processes and problems. J.L. Barkas, Assistant Professor at New York Institute of Technology, has done research on friendship patterns among young, urban, single women. This book is a continuation of her research interests into friendships of other categories of individuals as well—married women, males, children, adolescents, and the elderly. It includes the important and representative works, both published and unpublished, and contains audio-visual and organizational resources. The multidisciplinary content and an emphasis on sociological works make this reference book useful to both specialists and non-specialists alike.

Dan. A. Chekki
University of Winnipeg

INTRODUCTION

In the last ten years, more studies on friendship have been conducted, and more research has been published or presented at professional meetings, than in the previous fifty years. Introductory sociology courses and textbooks are beginning to reflect this new emphasis on friendship and such related subjects as self-disclosure, trust, same-sex intimacy, conflict, networks, and popularity.

Many reasons have been advanced for the resurgence of interest in friendship, a relationship so valued in ancient times that Aristotle, Cicero, and Plato, among others, devoted treatises or dialogues to it (see entries 9, 63, 222). Most of the explanations for the increased attention to friendship rest on recent social changes. What are some of those changes?

A pattern of later first marriage, delayed parenting, and increased life expectancy is a common one in Western cultures today. Marriage, in some socioeconomic groups, is being delayed until the late twenties or early thirties, or avoided altogether (see entries 17, 20, 139, and 572). If young adults leave home, especially if they relocate to distant communities, they consider friendship ties more important for longer periods than those who move directly from their nuclear family of orientation to their own family of procreation. Thus the delaying of first marriage, as well as the increase in singleness after divorce (between marriages), has contributed to the value of friendship for intimacy and companionship. Because of the longer life expectancy of men and women today, there is also more time after the children have left home, or after the death of a spouse, when friendship may fulfill some of the needs once met by offspring or partner (see entry 232).

The increase of working women in higher professional positions has caused them to reexamine their early sex role socialization and to question whether office friendships, especially close ones, are appropriate or beneficial (see entries 393 and 423). Furthermore, the women's movement, with its emphasis on "sisterhood," has revived interest in female friendships; it has also inspired men to reevaluate their own same-sex relationships (see entries 558 and 566). Part of the motivation to their renewed interest in friendship is that their wives, whom they had come to rely on as their best friends, are now also working and dividing their energies beyond their family (see entry 530).

The increased mobility that is pervasive in contemporary societies makes it necessary to quickly learn how to initiate and sustain new friendships since childhood friends and old classmates or colleagues are left behind. If more accessible friendships are not added to those old ties, loneliness results (see entry 122).

As Hugh C. Foot, Willard W. Hartup, Zick Rubin, Robert L. Selman, and others have shown, friendship is important even in infancy; peer relations serve to build (or shatter) self-esteem and competence in the developing child (see entries 101, 236, 430, and 559). No longer is friendship viewed as essential only during adolescence, when a youth is establishing his or her own identity and pulling away from parental and sibling influences (see entry 262). The meaning of friendship in the middle years is being investigated; rather than being a threat to a marriage, friendship can decrease the pressure on the couple to be everything to each other, taking some of the strain off their intimate dyad (research being conducted by the author on marriage and friendship). Marjorie Fisk Lowenthal, Clayton Haven, Irving Rosow, Zena Blau, and others have already documented the fact that friendship is essential to the emotional well-being of the elderly (see entries 37, 232, and 490).

There are definite problems in researching friendship, obstacles that some researchers have been trying to address, but a collective effort is necessary if those dilemmas are to be solved (see entries 4, 18, and 350). The first problem is in the definition of *friendship*. Marriage is easy enough to define, but what is friendship? Does it encompass casual business friends, as well as a definite "best" friendship? What does it mean if someone calls someone a "friend" or even a "close friend"? The second problem is in trying to establish norms for friendship: How many friends can any person handle before those relationships wane in value because of competing demands? How often should one see a friend? Talk on the phone? Write, if far away? Was Montaigne correct when he wrote that one could have only one best friend for, if one had two such friends, and both were in need, to which would one turn (see entry 504)? Or was Georg Simmel right when he said the complexity of modern life necessitated differentiated friendships, whereby no one friend was "best," but numerous friends provided this or that emotional or experiential benefit (see entry 252)?

This bibliography developed from the references that I consulted during the three years I researched my doctoral dissertation, "Friendship Patterns Among Young Urban Single Women" (see entry 17). An additional year was spent completing a booklet on friendship throughout the life cycle, as well as further research for this bibliography and for a work-in-progress developed from my dissertation (see entry 18). My original dissertation bibliography, as well as the sources I learned about after its completion, were gathered through a variety of means, such as making computerized searches (in sociology, psychology, anthropology, literature, philosophy, and history), as well as checking the citations in other friendship works, contacting friendship (and loneliness) experts, such as Steve Duck, Zick Rubin, Ralph Potter, Nicholas Babchuck, Daniel Perlman, Letitia Anne Peplau, J. Barry Gurdin, for suggestions, and even placing a notice for scholars to contact me in *Footnotes*, the newsletter published by the American Sociological Association (see entries 615 and 642).

It is impossible to thank all the social scientists, other scholars, and friends who generously mailed reprints to me, sent me copies of papers presented at conferences, or just talked with me about friendship and the work they were doing, or suggested names of others whom I should contact. Their names do appear in this bibliography as part of the citations for their related published or unpublished works. Although I take full credit or blame for this friendship bibliography, it is, by the nature of its presentation, a collective effort by living and dead writers and thinkers and I am sincerely grateful to those who knowingly or unknowingly contributed to this final document. In addition to the social scientists singled out above, I want to thank Jose Schorr, a lawyer and writer, for providing copies of the journal articles on the lawyer as friend that appear in this bibliography and Don Wigal for the citations that he provided.

Although this bibliography is part of the Garland Bibliographies in Sociology series, and the emphasis is on sociological works, it became clear to me that an interdisciplinary approach was necessary. The reasons are self-evident to anyone who has pondered friendship: it is reflected in the interdisciplinary nature of the *Journal of Social and Personal Relationships*, edited by Steve Duck, a psychologist and pioneer in this field, and in the varied backgrounds of the conference participants at the First and Second International Conferences on Personal Relationships, held in 1982 and 1984 at the University of Wisconsin at Madison (see entries 146–50, 653, and 690).

Not only do the demands of the study of friendship necessitate an interdisciplinary bibliography, but selected references from such diverse areas as divorce, marriage, aging, child development, and sex role socialization also have to be included. Nor can this bibliography be definitive; new research is being conducted and new findings are going to press even as this bibliography is completed. Thus the bibliography is only as comprehensive as I could make it at this time. It is also selective, although I have tried to include the seminal works on friendship, whatever the discipline. Inclusion in or exclusion from this bibliography is not reflective of an endorsement or condemnation by this researcher. When appropriate, annotations of varying lengths are provided that interpret, critique, or simply report on the findings of those friendship-related materials.

J.L.B.
September 27, 1984

FRIENDSHIP

BOOKS, BOOKLETS, DISSERTATIONS, AND REPORTS

1. Adams, Margaret. <u>Single Blessedness: Observations on the Single Status in Married Society</u>. New York: Penguin Books, 1978.

    This is an expansion of social worker Adams' 1971 journal article on single women (which had a discussion of their friendship patterns). Adams' book-length study is based on 27 in-depth interviews with unmarried men and women living in Boston, Philadelphia, and New York. The author reports on how her respondents defined friendship, how their definitions related to their social class, as well as male-female and homosexual friendships.

2. Alger, William Rouseville. <u>The Friendships of Women</u>. Boston: Roberts Brothers, 1868.

3. Allan, Graham A. "Friendship and Kinship." Unpublished Ph.D. thesis, University of Essex, 1976.

4. _____. <u>A Sociology of Friendship and Kinship</u>. London: George Allen & Unwin, 1979.

    British sociologist Allan introduces the results of his own research based on interviews with 50 men and women, all but two were married pairs, with a general review of the sociological literature on kinship and friendship. Allan makes the following interesting observations: most sociologists (up to that time), when discussing friendship, talk about friendship in general, although their research is usually based upon the answers of respondents to questions only about close friends; the quantitative measure of frequency of contact with a friend, is usually the factor (but not necessarily a reliable one), in determining closeness. Although the difference between a blood relation and a marital relation -- the two types of kinship -- are quite clear, the difference between a close friend and a "friend" are not easily discerned. Allan does note, however, that it is rarely someone met in an institutional setting -- e.g., the work environment -- who is referred to as a friend, unless that relationship voluntarily continues on the outside on a nonutilitarian basis.

Allan defined friendship as a "personal" relationship in three connected senses. The author's orientation to friendship is that of symbolic interactionism. However, Allan restates the exchange perspective, stressing that exchange is part of friendship if this condition exists: "Friends can quite legitimately make use of one another in instrumental ways without threatening the relationship, provided that it is clear that they are being used because they are friends and not friends because they are useful." Allan concludes his nine-page discussion of "Aspects of Friendship in Western Culture" with the view that "friendship is a relationship between equals," a notion that he sees as closely tied to the idea of reciprocity, and the idea that friendship involves mutually labelling each other as friends.

5. Argyle, Michael. Social Interaction. London: Methuen, 1969.

6. _____ and Henderson, Monika. Anatomy of Friendship. London: Heinemann, 1984. (in press)

7. Aries, Philippe. Centuries of Childhood: A Social History of Family Life. Translated by Robert Baldick. New York: Vintage Books, 1962.

   Historian Aries' well-known thesis is that before the seventeenth century, an open family system existed of kin, friends, and visitors; until they were old enough to be dealt with as little adults, children were largely ignored. The child-centered nuclear family emerged after that. On friendship in seventeenth century literature, see page 376.

8. _____. Western Attitudes Toward Death from the Middle Ages to the Present. Translated by Patricia M. Ranum. Baltimore: Johns Hopkins University Press, 1974.

   Aries traces the change in the "death scene." During the Middle Ages, death was a "public ceremony....It is essential that parents, friends, and neighbors be present."

Between 1930 and 1950, the death site was displaced so that "One no longer died at home in the bosom of one's family" and friends, but alone in a hospital.

9. Aristotle. Aristotle in Twenty-Three Volumes. Vol. 19: The Nicomachean Ethics. Translated by H. Rackham. Books 8 and 9. Cambridge: Harvard University Press, 1968.

    Except for Cicero's essay, this is one of the most comprehensive of the early philosophical treatises on friendship. Aristotle considered friendship a "virtue;" friendship is only possible when there is "mutual" "goodwill." Both friends must be aware of this goodwill and "the cause of their goodwill must be one of the loveable" three traits -- "good," "pleasant," or "useful." According to Aristotle, friendships based on pleasure or utility are most easily dissolved for what is pleasant and useful about someone may change. The best and most lasting form of friendship is that based on goodness, "a permanent quality." Aristotle notes that genuine friendship takes time; potential friends must learn if each is worthy of friendship. Separation will not completely end a friendship, although "it prevents its active exercise." Equality is a necessary ingredient for friendship; if a disparity of wealth, vice, or virtue arises, the friendship will probably end. It is important to note, however, when Aristotle writes about a friend as "another self," and indeed throughout his treatise, it is only a best or very close friend that his thoughts apply to (not to casual or, as Simmel termed them, to "differentiated friendships").

10. Asher, Steve and Gottman, John, editors. The Development of Children's Friendships. Cambridge: Cambridge University Press, 1981.

    See William A. Corsaro, "Friendship in the Nursery School: Social Organization in a Peer Environment."

11. Augustine. The Confessions of St. Augustine, Bishop of Hippo. Translated by E.B. Pusey. New York: Dutton, 1951.

    See Book IV, paragraphs 1-24, pages 54-72.

12. Bachrach, Leona L. "Marital Status and Mental Disorder: An Analytical Review." U.S. Department of Health, Education, and Welfare, Public Health Service, Series D., No. 3. Washington, D.C.: U.S. Government Printing Office, 1975.

   A survey of the social science research on marital status and mental hospital admissions.

13. Bald, R. C. <u>Literary Friendship in the Age of Wordsworth</u>. New York: Octagon, 1968.

14. Baehr, Consuelo. <u>Best Friends</u>. New York: Delacorte Press, 1980. (<u>Fiction</u>)

   A novel about a friendship triad at boarding school and their meeting eighteen years later.

15. Ballweg, John A. "Social Class Differences in Friend and Kin Relationships of the Negro Conjugal Unit." Unpublished Ph.D. thesis, University of Nebraska (Lincoln), 1967.

16. Barkas, J.L. <u>Creative Time Management</u>. Englewood Cliffs, N.J.: Prentice-Hall, 1984.

   Finding time for friends, as well as how to efficiently socialize or entertain, are discussed, with practical tips, in chapter 6, "Improving Your Personal Time Management."

17. _____. "Friendship Patterns Among Young Urban Single Women." Unpublished Ph.D. thesis, City University of New York, 1983.

   Extensive in-person interviews were conducted with women between the ages of twenty and forty who were living alone on one randomly selected block on the Upper East Side of Manhattan. The friendship patterns of this sample (N = 27) were analyzed and interpreted, with some of the findings contradicting the literature about female friendships. Of the fifty closest and failed friendships discussed in detail by this sample, only two friendships ended because of rivalry over men. For the current closest friendships of this sample, 41% are dyads, 22% are triads, and the remainder are networks. There are, on average, 1 best, 4 close, 8 casual, and 2 failed friendships for this sample population. A major finding of this study was that the social integration of this sample of single women was generally high not because they had one all-encompassing "great" friendship, but because they were involved in a variety of non-romantic relationships, such as dyadic, triadic, or network friendships of varying levels of intimacy (casual, close, or best friendships), work-related acquaintanceships, and close relationships with nuclear or extended kin members who were described as "like a friend" (friendly kin relations).

18. _____. "Friendship Throughout Life." New York: Public Affairs Committee, 1983.

This booklet defines friendship and discusses why it is important. Gender differences in friendship patterns are presented as well as summaries of key research on friendship throughout the life cycle (childhood, adolescence, married years, older singles, old age). Quotations from the author's original research, as well as secondary sources, are used to illustrate major points.

19. _____. The Help Book. New York: Scribner's, 1979.

An annotated guide to help in 52 areas of concern, from alcoholism to volunteerism, providing local, state, and national organizations, and government agencies, as well as reviews of published references and audio-visual materials. In addition to providing information and referrals to direct services, networking (and friendship) are goals of most of the dozens of self-help organizations listed in this directory.

20. _____. Single in America. New York: Atheneum, 1980.

In this study of single men and women (never-marrieds, once-marrieds, and widowed), friendship was found to be a fundamental social relation in lieu of, or in addition to, romantic or family ties.

21. _____. *Victims*. New York: Scribner's, 1978.

    This study of the effects of violent personal and property crime on the victim and his or her family and friends also deals with the responses of friends to victimization. See pages xi, 17, 36-7.

22. Barnes, J. A. *Social Networks*. Reading, MA: Addison-Wesley, 1972, Module in Anthropology, No. 26, pp. 1-29.

23. Bell, Robert R. *Worlds of Friendship*. Beverly Hills: Sage, 1981.

    Sociologist Bell writes that friendship has become more significant in modern American society "because of the weakening of many kinship ties" and that "...as the emotional ties and rewards through the family are reduced other relationships are needed." Included are chapters on friendship as it relates to childhood and adolescence, women, men, cross-sex friendship, courtship, marriage, divorce, and the elderly.

24. Belmont, David Eugene. "Early Greek Guest Friendship and Its Role in Homer's Odyssey." Unpublished Ph.D. thesis, Princeton University, 1962.

25. Benedict, Ruth. *Patterns of Culture*. Preface by Margaret Mead. Boston: Houghton Mifflin, 1934, 1959.

    In social anthropologist Benedict's classic report on the Pueblos of New Mexico, the Dobuans of New Guinea, and the Indians of the Northwest Coast of America, the emphasis is on puberty and marriage and divorce customs, rather than friendship. However, there are some references to friendship. Benedict writes, for example: "Behind a show of friendship, behind the evidences of co-operation, in every field of life, the Dobuan believes that he has only treachery to expect." (page 171)

26. Bensman, Joseph and Lilienfeld, Robert. <u>Between Public and Private: The Lost Boundaries of the Self</u>. New York: Free Press, 1979.

   The authors, who are sociologists, call intimacy, including friendship, "...a safety-value for the self."

27. Berger, Peter L. <u>Invitation to Sociology: A Humanistic Perspective</u>. Garden City, N.Y.: Anchor Press/Doubleday, 1963.

   The author's brief analysis of marriage, from a sociological rather than a popular perspective, suggests some of the considerations a sociologist analyzing friendship should explore.

28. _____ and Kellner, Hansfried. <u>Sociology Reinterpreted: An Essay on Method and Vocation</u>. Garden City, N.Y.: Anchor Press/Doubleday, 1981.

   The sociological interpretation of man as one influenced by social control can be applied to culturally determined definitions of friendship and friendship choices that individuals make; "...there is no bonding between human beings without the effect of boundedness." (See especially chapter 4, "Sociological Interpretation and the Problem of Freedom.")

29. _____ and Luckmann, Thomas. <u>The Social Construction of Reality</u>. Garden City, N.Y.: Doubleday, 1966.

30. Berkowitz, S.D. and Wellman, Barry. <u>Structural Sociology</u>. Cambridge: Cambridge University Press, 1984. (in press)

   A discussion of social networks and community structure.

31. Bernard, Jessie. <u>The Future of Marriage</u>. New York:

Bantam Books, 1973.

A popular book by the notable sociologist that introduced the concept of the "his and hers" marriage, unfortuately lacking in a discussion of the effect of marriage on friendship.

32. Berne, Eric. Games People Play: The Psychology of Human Relationships. New York: Grove Press, 1964.

Psychiatrist Berne presents his Transactional Analysis approach to interpersonal relationships. On friendships, see page 55.

33. Bernikow, Louise. Among Women. New York: Harmony Books, 1980.

Poet and critic Bernikow draws on history and biographical accounts of literary figures to discuss female relationships. Chapter 4, "Friends," highlights the friendship essays of Bacon, Emerson, and Taylor, concentrating on the friendship of authors Virginia Woolf and Katherine Mansfield.

34. Berscheid, Ellen and Walster, Elaine Hatfield. Interpersonal Attraction. Reading, MA: Addison-Wesley, 1969.

35. Black, Hugh. Friendship. Chicago: Revell, 1903.

36. Blau, Peter M. Exchange and Power in Social Life. New York: Wiley, 1964.

A classic original social exchange approach to relationships, developed from the works of Simmel, Goffman, Weber, and Parsons. Blau's explorations of making a favorable first impression, reciprocity in relationships, expectations, and the dynamics of change and adjustment in groups all have implications for friendship. On friends, see pages 20, 26-7, 31-3, 36, 38, 88-9, 103-4, 105, 107, and 143. Written in the general theoretical style of Simmel, Blau's book is well-written and supported with some examples, although support from specific research would strengthen the book's propositions.

37. Blau, Zena Smith. Old Age in a Changing Society. New York: Franklin Watts, 1973.

Blau, like Irving Rosow, discovered through her original research on the elderly that just one close friendship can reduce the depression and loneliness that often accompany retirement or widowhood. Relationships with grown children, no matter how frequent, do not compensate for the reductions in peer relations subsequent to those role exits (although the elderly do turn to their family members in times of financial need or when they are physically ill). (See, especially, chapter 4, "The Significance of Friendship" and chapter 5, "Structural Constraints on Friendship".)

38. _____. "Old Age: A Study of Change in Status". Unpublished Ph.D. thesis, Columbia University, 1957.

39. Block, Joel D. Friendship. New York: Macmillan, 1980.

Intended for a general audience, this book summarizes the results of clinical psychologist Block's national questionnaire survey of 2,063 adult men and women. A copy of Block's 52-question survey is included. In addition to same- and opposite-sex friendships, the author discusses marriage and friendship, divorce and friendship, friendship and fame, and the fundamental ingredients for a successful friendship.

40. Blum, Alan F. and McHugh, Peter, eds. Friends, Enemies, and Strangers: Theorizing in Art, Science, and Everyday Life. Norwood, N.J.: Ablex, 1979.

41. Blum, Lawrence A. Friendship, Altruism, and Morality. London: Routledge & Kegan Paul, 1981.

42. Boissevain, Jeremy. Friends of Friends: Networks, Manipulators and Coalitions. New York: St. Martin's Press,

1974.

43. _____ and Mitchell, J. Clyde. Network Analysis: Studies in Human Interaction. The Hague: Mouton, 1973.

44. Bok, Sissela. Lying: Moral Choice in Public and Private Life. New York: Pantheon Books, 1978.

   Bok distinguishes between lying and deception, both considerations in an understanding of friendship. See "Letters of Recommendation," pages 68-70, on the ethics of "inflated" letters "to give extra praise to a friend." Provocative but not as richly illustrated as Bok's next book, Secrets (see review below).

45. _____. Secrets: On the Ethics of Concealment and Revelation. New York: Vintage Books, 1984.

   Secrecy, and self-disclosure, components of intimate friendships, and important concepts to an understanding of friendship, are probed in detail in Bok's thought-provoking and well-researched book. See pages 38, 41, and 43 for specific references on how secrecy applies to friendship.

46. Bolotin, David. Plato's Dialogue on Friendship: An Interpretation of the Lysis, With a New Translation. Ithaca, N.Y.: Cornell University Press, 1979.

47. Booth, G. A Friend is Friendly! Norwalk, CT.: C.R. Gibson, 1981.

48. Bott, Elizabeth. Family and Social Network: Roles, Norms, and External Relationships in Ordinary Urban Families. London: Tavistock, 1957.

   Bott is credited with the first analytical use of the concept of the social network. Bott and her colleagues interviewed twenty London families, seeking to find out the varying ways that conjugal roles were performed and the types of external social relationships that they had (loose-knit, medium-knit, or close-knit networks).

49. Brain, Robert. *Friends and Lovers.* New York: Basic Books, 1976.

    In "Whistling in the Dark," Anatole Broyard's October 5, 1976 *New York Times* (p. 43) review of anthropologist Brain's book, Broyard writes: "Our 'whole person,' as we now consider ourselves, is often regarded as halved by friendship, but doubled by love. Love is the great magnifier, writes Mr. Brain, and friendship is often treated as a mere interim activity while we rest from our ardors. Like aggression and hate, love has glamour, while friendship is all too often conceived as a mere leak in our sense of privacy....While love and sex are great upstagers, our sanity and our happiness may rest more firmly on a foundation of friendship."
    Some of the chapters in *Friends and Lovers* most pertinent to a study of friendship are: Friends in Blood, Lopsided Friendships, Business Friends, Friends in Common, and All the Lonely People.

50. Brenton, Myron. *Friendship.* New York: Stein and Day, 1975.

51. Broderick, Carlfred Bartholomew. "Predicting Friendship Behavior: A Study of the Determinants of Friendship Selection and Maintenance in a College Population." Unpublished Ph.D. thesis, Cornell University, 1956.

52. Brown, Helen Gurley. *Having It All.* New York: Simon & Schuster, 1982.

    Cosmopolitan magazine editor Brown devotes a chapter to "Friends" in her popular advice book on love, sex, money, and happiness.

53. Bry, Adelaide. *Friendship: How to Have a Friend and How to Be a Friend.* New York: Grosset and Dunlap, 1979.

54. Buber, Martin. *I and Thou.* Translated by Walter Kaufmann. New York: Scribner's, 1970.

Kaufman notes in his introduction the differences among I-I, I-It, It-It, We-We, Us-Them, and philosopher Buber's I-Thou. "Relation is reciprocity," Buber writes, "...without It a human being cannot live. But whoever lives only with that is not human." Buber uses the du (you) that in German is an expression of intimacy for close friends and lovers.

55. Burton, Charles Emory. "Friendship Patterns of Professionals: A Study of Scientists and Engineers." Unpublished Ph.D. thesis, University of Tennessee, 1976.

56. Cargan, Leonard and Melko, Matthew. Preface by John Scanzoni. Singles: Myths and Realities. Beverly Hills: Sage, 1982. (Published in cooperation with the National Council on Family Relations.)

Based on 400 interviews with residents of the Dayton, Ohio metropolitan area, the authors report on the results of their 77 "mostly closed-ended" self-administered questionnaire items. In addition to a chapter on loneliness, there is specific mention of friendship in the chapters on leisure time (pages 83-85) and happiness (pages 166-7).

57. Carnegie, Dale. How to Win Friends and Influence People. New York: Pocket Books, 1940.

This is the continuously popular best seller by Carnegie, who started his first human relations courses in the early 1900s, initially published in 1936. Includes chapters on how to make people like you, fundamental techniques in handling people, methods of persuasion, how to write effective letters, and rules for having a happier life.

58. Carpenter, Edward. Iolaus: An Anthology of Friendship. Boston: Godspeed, 1902.

A collection of philosophical and literary references to friendship in pre-Christian and Greek times as well as ealy Christian, medieval, Renaissance, and modern periods.

59. Cary, David MacKenzie. "Attitudes Toward Authority, Friend Choice, and Delinquency." Unpublished Ph.D. thesis, University of Minnesota, 1975.

60. Chambliss, William Joseph. "The Selection of Friends." Unpublished Ph.D. thesis, Indiana University, 1962.

61. Chasin, Gerald. "A Study of the Determinants of Friendship Choice and of the Content of the Friendship Relationship." Unpublished Ph.D. thesis, University of Iowa, 1968.

62. Chelune, Gordon, ed. Self-Disclosure. San Francisco: Jossey-Bass, 1979.

63. Cicero. On Old Age and On Friendship. Translated by Frank O. Copley. Ann Arbor: University of Michigan Press, 1967.

    Cicero stresses many of the same themes that Aristotle did in his friendship treatise, such as: man is a social creature who needs friends; "friendship can exist only between good men." Cicero empathically states the universality and necessity of friendship: "Friendship, as you know, is the one thing in human life which all men with one voice agree is worthwhile." Like Aristotle, Cicero writes that virtue is the first ingredient for friendship, and self-sufficiency, like Aristotle's self-love, must precede friendship. Cicero emphasizes that potential friendships should be initiated slowly -- the potential friend should be tested along the way -- for once a friendship is developed, it should not be broken. If a friendship does end, however, it is important to avoid being at war with your ex-friend. Better to let the friendship fade than to have an enemy. "For there is nothing more unseemly than openly to enter the lists against someone with whom you have lived on terms of intimacy," Cicero writes. In summary, Cicero states that friendship requires respect, virtuous men, and honesty.

64. Cohen, Bernard P. "The Relationship of Social and Personal Attributes to Friendship Choices." Unpublished

Honors Thesis, Harvard University, 1951.

65. Cohen, Steven Martin. "Patterns of Inter-ethnic Marriage and Friendship in the United States." Unpublished Ph.D. thesis, Columbia University, 1974.

66. Cott, Nancy. The Bonds of Womanhood. New Haven: Yale University Press, 1977.

   Basing her conclusions on women's diaries and minister's sermons, historian Cott's conclusions are probably most applicable to literate, white, middle-class, American-born, Protestant New Englanders of the 19th century. Still her findings in chapter 5, "Sisterhood," are intriguing as a historical exploration of friendship at a time when, according to Cott, there was a "newly self-conscious and idealized concept of female friendship." Friendship, it seemed, offered a relationship based on equality in contrast to the subordination common in marriages of that time.

67. Crader, Kelly Wayne. "Homophily of Adolescent Friendship Relations: A Contextual Analysis." Unpublished Ph.D. thesis, Emory University, 1971.

68. Damon, William. The Social World of the Child. San Francisco: Jossey-Bass, 1977.

69. Davidson, Laurie and Gordon, Laura Kramer. The Sociology of Gender. Chicago: Rand McNally, 1979.

   A discussion of sex role socialization that provides a background to the gender differences in friendship patterns that emerge in adult men and women. See especially pages 22, 29, 32, 206, and 255.

70. Davis, Murray S. Intimate Relations. New York: Free Press, 1973.

   Based on Davis' general observations and his theoretical orientation as a symbolic interactionist, Davis includes friendship as one of the three types of intimate relations that he describes (the other two being lovers and

spouses). Davis deals with the impulses and needs that
drive a couple to become acquaintances, rather than
strangers, and to be together, rather than apart. At each
stage of his developmental view of intimacy -- a
relationship on a compendium from total strangeness to
complete familiarity -- there are possible complications
that may lead the couple temporarily or permanently part.
Like Simmel, Davis is concerned with the relevation of
secrets, and all the benefits and difficulties that those
disclosures may provoke. According to Davis, exchanges
(favors) figure heavily in evolving relationships; physical
and psychological ones are extended with the possible
resulting complications: "(1) <u>assurance</u> of forthcoming
favors; (2) <u>dependence</u> on current favors and (3) <u>obligation</u>
for past favors."

71. Dawley, Harold H. <u>Friendship: How to Make & Keep Friends.</u>
Englewood Cliffs, N.J.: Prentice-Hall, 1980.

    A psychologist's popular treatment of the topic, based
on the notion that friendship is "one of the best way to
overcome" loneliness.

72. Day, Barbara Ruth. "The Relationship of Need Patterns to
Selection in the Formation of Courtship Couples and Same-Sex
Friendships." Unpublished Ph.D. thesis, University of
Washington, 1956.

73. de Beauvoir, Simone. <u>The Second Sex.</u> New York: Bantam
Books, 1961.

74. Degler, Carl N. <u>At Odds: Women and the Family in America
from the Revolution to the Present.</u> New York: Oxford
University Press, 1980.

    Although historian Degler's primary emphasis is the
evolution of marriage and the family in the United States
since the 19th century, there is some discussion of the
women's sphere and of friendship among women (see pages
144-51).

75. Derlega, Valerian and Winstead, B., eds. <u>Friendship: A
Sourcebook.</u> New York: Springer Verlag, 1985 (<u>in press</u>).

76. _____ and Chaikin, Alan. Sharing Intimacy. Englewood Cliffs, N.J.: Prentice-Hall, 1975.

See especially the chapters on self-disclosure and friendship.

77. Dowling, Colette. The Cinderella Complex. New York: Simon & Schuster, 1981.

The best seller about the syndrome whereby a woman believes a man will "save her" from her responsibilities, and tailors all her work and relationships to him. The concept is something to consider when analyzing the reported tendency of some women to give up their friends when a man comes into their life, or, after they marry, when his friends become more pivotal to their social life than hers.

78. Duck, Steve. Friends, For Life: The Psychology of Close Relationships. New York: St. Martin's Press, 1983.

Psychologist Duck, a leading authority on friendship, details the reasons friends are important as well as the stages through which friendship evolves. A chapter on children's friendships is also included as well as a discussion of relationship problems.

79. _____. Personal Relationships and Personal Constructs: A Study of Friendship Formation. New York: Wiley, 1973.

80. _____. The Study of Acquaintance. Hampshire, England: Gower, 1977.

81. _____, ed. Personal Relationships 4: Dissolving Personal Relationships. London: Academic Press, 1982.

82. _____, ed. Personal Relationships 5: Repairing Personal Relationships. London: Academic Press, 1984.

See especially the chapter by Sidney Cobb and Jessie Jones-Cobb on social support and health.

83. _____ and Gilmour, Robin, eds. <u>Personal Relationships 1: Studying Personal Relationships.</u> New York: Academic Press, 1981.

84. _____. <u>Personal Relationships 2: Developing Personal Relationships.</u> New York: Academic Press, 1981.

 Specifically on friendship, see: W. Dickens and D. Perlman, "Friendship Over the Life Cycle"; J. La Gaipa, "Children's Friendships"; I. Kon, "Adolescent Friendships: Some Unanswered Questions for Future Research"; J. Reisman, "Adult Friendships"; and S. Chown, "Friendship in Old Age."

85. _____. <u>Personal Relationships 3: Personal Relationships in Disorder.</u> New York: Academic Press, 1981.

 See J. La Gaipa and D. Wood, "Friendship in Disturbed Adolescents" and D. Perlman and L. Peplau, "Toward a Social Psychology of Loneliness."

86. _____ and Perlman, Daniel. <u>Understanding Personal Relationships: An Interdisciplinary Approach.</u> London: Sage, 1984. (in press) (Sage Series on Personal Relationships, Vol. 1)

 See especially the chapter by Barry Wellman on "Sex, Work, and Networks." Other chapters include: Dan P. McAdams, "A Motivational Approach to the Study of Friendship" and Phillip Shaver, Wyndol Furman, and Duane Buhrmester, "Aspects of a Life Transition: Network Changes, Social Skills, and Loneliness."

87. Durkheim, Emile. <u>The Division of Labor in Society.</u> Translated by George Simpson. New York: Free Press, 1964.

 There is a brief discussion of friendship in this work. Durkheim presents both points of view about friendship, such as "Difference, as likeness, can be a cause of mutual attraction and one may seek out in a friend qualities or services that an individual lacks."

88. _____. Suicide: A Study in Sociology. Translated by John A. Spauldin and George Simpson. Edited with an introduction by George Simpson. London: Routledge & Kegan Paul, 1952; reprint ed. 1972.

89. Edwards, Marie and Hoover, Eleanor. The Challenge of Being Single. New York: Signet Books, 1974.

90. Embree, John F. Suye Mura: A Japanese Village. Chicago: University of Chicago Press, 1939.

   A discussion of the importance placed on age in the friendships of Japanese boys and men.

91. Epstein, Joseph. Divorced in America. New York: Penguin Books, 1974.

   A first-person report, enhanced by statistics and discussions of social trends beyond the author's experience, on divorce, including how friends aid or hinder during the disengagement phases.

92. Epstein, Joyce and Karweit, Nancy L., eds. Friends in School: Patterns in Selection and Influence in Secondary Schools. New York: Academic Press, 1983.

   A collection by sociologists and psychologists on three aspects of peer group research -- theory, selection, and influence. Chapters include: "Friends Among Students in Schools: Environmental and Developmental Factors"; "School Organization and Friendship Selection"; "Examining Theories of Adolescent Friendships"; "Sex Differences in Adolescent Relationships: Friendship and Status"; and "Commentary: The Relationship Between Friendship Selection and Peer Influence."

93. Erikson, Erik H. Childhood and Society, 2nd ed. New York: Norton, 1950, 1963.

   In stage 5, "Identity vs. Role Confusion" in "Eight

Ages of Man," psychoanalyst Erikson discusses why, for some adolescents, their friendships may seem poor choices, at least by adult standards. Cliques and stereotyping are factors influencing these friendship choices.

94. _____. Identity and the Life Cycle. New York: International Universities Press, 1959.

95. Faderman, Lillian. Surpassing the Love of Men: Romantic Friendship and Love Between Women from the Renaissance to the Present. New York: Morrow, 1981.

    A study that includes romantic friendships, a term coined during the eighteenth century to describe intense, commited friendships, most often without sexual involvement, between women who had married for economic reasons, and whose same-sex friendships emotionally sustained.

96. Fasteau, Marc Feigen. The Male Machine. New York: Delta Books, 1975.

97. Feinberg, Paul. Friends. New York: Quick Fox, 1980.

    A photo essay of short interviews about friendships between the famous (and the not-so-famous) and their friends. Includes Art Buchwald and his friend Harry, a pharmacist, Sugar Ray Leonard and Joe, a security guard, actor Jack Warden, a homemaker, a newspaper correspondent, and others. It's interesting that the friendship dyads are categorized by Feinberg by the occupational status of its members.

98. Fischer, Claude S. To Dwell Among Friends: Personal Networks in Town and City. Chicago: University of Chicago, 1982.

    Based on interviews with more than 1,250 persons in fifty northern California communities, this is a study of "how urban life changes personal relations and the ways people think and act socially: such matters as friendship, intimacy, involvement in the community, and life-style."

99. Fischer, Claude S.; Jackson, Robert Max; Stueve, C. Ann; Gerson, Kathleen; Jones, Lynne McCallister with Baldassare, Mark. <u>Networks and Places: Social Relations in an Urban Setting.</u> New York: Free Press, 1977.

100. Fiske, Adele M. <u>The Survival and Development of the Ancient Concept of Friendship in the Early Middle Ages.</u> Cuernavaca, Mexico: Centro Intercultural de Documentacion, 1970.

101. Foot, H. C.; Chapman, A. J.; and Smith, J. R., eds. <u>Friendship and Social Relations in Children.</u> London: Wiley, 1980.

 Includes Deborah Lowe Vandell and Edward Mueller's, "Peer Play and Friendships During the First Two Years."

102. Fortier, T. L. "On Friendship: Its Nature, Kinds, and Effects in Human Life." Unpublished Ph.D. thesis, l'Universite Laval, 1970.

103. Freud, Anna. <u>The Ego and the Mechanisms of Defense.</u> Revised edition. New York: International Universities Press, 1966.

 See pages 167-72 for friendships in adolescence.

104. Friedman, Edward Philip. "Friendship Choice and Clique Formation in a Home for the Aged." Unpublished Ph.D. thesis, Yale University, 1966.

105. Fromm, Erich. <u>The Art of Loving.</u> New York: Harper & Row, 1956, 1974.

 A simplification of psychoanalyst Fromm's thesis is that one must love oneself before one can love another. Fromm does not, however, consider if the act of loving, or being someone's friend, can teach the self-love one lacks. Fromm is most concerned with romantic love, but also brings in friendship (as well as parent-child and love of God). "Without love, humanity could not exist for a day," Fromm

writes. "In contrast to symbiotic union, mature <u>love is
union under the condition of preserving one's integrity,
one's individuality</u>."

106. Gans, Herbert. <u>Urban Villagers</u>. New York: Free Press, 1962.

107. Gay, F. <u>The Friendship Book</u>. London: D.C. Thomson, 1975.

108. Gelven, Michael. <u>Winter, Friendship, Guilt: Sources of Self-Inquiry</u>. New York: Harper Torchbooks, 1972.

109. Gibran, Kahlil. <u>The Prophet</u>. New York: Knopf, 1963.

    See "On Friendship," pages 58-9. Gibran notes that friendship should not be for opportunistic reasons but only "save the deepening of the spirit." "Laughter, and sharing of pleasures" are other qualities to seek in friendship.

110. Glaser, Barney G. and Straus, A.L. <u>Status Passages</u>. Chicago: Aldine, 1971.

111. Glazer-Melbin, Nona, ed. <u>Old Family/New Family: Interpersonal Relationships</u>. New York: D. Van Nostrand, 1975.

    Includes Joseph H. Pleck's chapter on men's friendships and intimacy problems, "Man to Man: Is Brotherhood Possible?" (For annotation, see listing in articles under <u>Pleck</u>.) Also includes Anne M. Seiden and Pauline B. Bart, "Woman to Woman: Is Sisterhood Powerful?" (See <u>Seiden</u> in articles section for annotation.)

112. Glick, Paul C. and Norton, Arthur J. <u>Marrying, Divorcing, and Living Together in the U.S. Today</u>. Washington, D.C.: Population Reference Bureau, October 1977.

    The increase in singleness of all types -- delaying of first marriage, increased divorce (and singleness between marriages), and living together (versus marriage) -- points to the heightened importance of friendship in contemporary America. Although the authors do not discuss friendship

directly, the trends that they cite and the statistical
data to substantiate their changes are notable in an
overview of the importance of friendship today.

113. Goethals, George W. and Klos, Dennis S. eds. Experiencing
Youth: First-Personal Accounts. 2nd ed. Boston: Little,
Brown, 1970, 1976.

114. Goffman, Erving. Behavior in Public Places: Notes on the
Social Organization of Gatherings. New York: Free Press,
1963.

   Includes chapters on acquaintanceship and communication
boundaries.

115. _____. Encounters: Two Studies in the Sociology of
Interaction. Indianapolis: Bobbs-Merrill Educational
Publishing, 1961.

   Includes symbolic interactionist Goffman's papers, "Fun
in Games" and "Role Distance."

116. _____. Interaction Ritual: Essays On Face-to-Face
Behavior. Garden City, N.Y.: Anchor Press/Doubleday, 1967.

117. _____. The Presentation of Self in Everyday Life.
Woodstock: Overlook Press, 1973.

118. _____. Stigma: Notes on the Management of Spoiled
Identity. Englewood Cliffs, N.J.: Prentice-Hall, 1963.

   Goffman's definition and descriptions of stigma might
be kept in mind in conducting friendship research since
respondents may minimize or avoid disclosing their failed
friendships if such an admission is viewed as stigmatizing.

119. Goldberg, Herb. The New Male: From Self-Destruction to
Self-Care. New York: New American Library, 1980.

   See pages 9, 24, 41, 213-4, 249 and 252 on the absence
of friendships among men, the importance of cultivating

intimate friendships, and business-related friendships.

120. Goode, William J. After Divorce. Glencoe, IL: Free Press, 1956.

   Goode's exhaustive and impressive study of the reasons for divorce among a large sample of women in Chicago might be considered in light of friendship, namely the length of time from meeting to marriage and the professed reasons for severing the marriage bond.

121. _____. The Family. Englewood Cliffs, N.J.: Prentice-Hall, 1964.

122. Gordon, Suzanne. Lonely in America. New York: Simon & Schuster, 1976.

   Gordon looks at loneliness in childhood and adolescence, singlehood, marriage, divorce, and old age. The urban environment and mobility (relocation as well as family disruption), characteristic of contemporary America, are seen as causes of the loneliness that Gordon suggests is a common problem today.

123. Gouldner, Helen Beem. "The Organization Woman: Patterns of Friendship and Organizational Commitment." Unpublished Ph.D. thesis, University of California, Los Angeles, 1960.

124. Greeley, Andrew M. The Friendship Game. Garden City, N.Y.: Doubleday, 1971.

125. Gruenberg, Sidonie with Hilda Sidney Krech. "Your Child's Friends". New York: Public Affairs Committee, 1959.

126. Gurdin, J. Barry. "Amitie/Friendship: The Socio-cultural Construction of Friendship in Contemporary Montreal." Unpublished Ph.D. thesis, University of Montreal, 1978.

127. Hagoel, Lea. "Urban Friendships: Qualitative and Quantitative Aspects of Primary Relations in an Urban Community Context." Unpublished Ph.D. thesis, University of Minnesota, 1980.

128. Hart, Nicky. *When Marriage Ends: A Study in Status Passage*. London: Tavistock, 1976.

    Based on this British sociologist's two-year participation in the Rivertown Association for the Divorced and Separated, as well as in-depth interviews with 63 men and women in the group, Hart explores the post-marriage experience, including networking and friendship patterns. On friendship, see especially pages 163, 164, 167-71, and 216.

129. Hearn, Janice W. *Making Friends, Keeping Friends*. Garden City, N.Y.: Doubleday, 1979.

130. Herrick, Shirley L. "Education and Friendship Formation." Unpublished Ph.D. thesis, University of Minnesota, 1971.

131. Hess, Beth B. "Friendship: A Study of Amicable Relationships of Middle-class, Middle-aged Managerial Migrants." Unpublished Ph.D. thesis, Rutgers, The State University of New Jersey (New Brunswick), 1971.

132. Hinde, Robert A. *Towards Understanding Relationships*. London: Academic Press, 1979.

133. Hoffman, Gerhard. "Interracial Fraternalization: Social Determinants of Friendship Relations Between Black and White Adolescents." Unpublished Ph.D. thesis, Purdue University, 1973.

134. Homans, George Caspar. *The Human Group*. New York: Harcourt, Brace, 1950.

135. _____. *Social Behavior: Its Elementary Forms*. Revised ed. New York: Harcourt Brace Jovanovich, 1974.

    Social exchange theorist Homans' general propositions about small group behavior and analyses of interpersonal relationships. On friendship and conformity, see pages 147-52; on friendship and proximity, see pages 144-45, 146.

136. Howard, Jane. *Families*. New York: Simon & Schuster, 1978.

Journalist Howard begins her account of a dozen or so families around the country with a quote from sociologist Robert Nisbet: "The family, not the individual, is the real molecule of society, the key link in the social chain of being." Howard also suggests that the single person has a family that includes his or her friends. Yet, unlike Lindsey's Friends as Family (see below), it is the blood tie that Howard writes about. "I always crave to meet my friends' relatives, and for that matter, my relatives' friends."

137. Howe, M. A. De Wolfe, Memories of a Hostess; A Chronicle of Friendships Drawn Chiefly from the Diaries of Mrs. James T. Fields. Salem, N.H.: Ayer, 1983. (Reprint of 1922 edition.)

138. Howell, Mary C. Helping Ourselves; Families and the Human Network. Boston: Beacon Press, 1975.

See chapter 4, "Weaving the Network," including a discussion of friends.

139. Hunt, Morton. The World of the Formerly Married. New York: McGraw-Hill, 1966.

140. _____ and Hunt, Bernice. The Divorce Experience. New York: McGraw-Hill, 1977.

Based on a nationwide survey and in-depth interviews, popular writers Hunt and Hunt explore the post-marriage separation and divorce experience, including attention to the reaction of friends to the news of the separation, as a way of meeting new people, and as a source of help.

141. Huston, Ted L. and Burgess, Robert L., eds. Social Exchange in Developing Relationships. Foreword by George C. Homans. New York: Academic Press, 1979.

142. Hutter, Horst. Politics as Friendship: The Origins of Classical Notions of Politics in the Theory and Practice of Friendship. Waterloo, Ontario: Wilfred Laurier University

Press, 1978.

143. James, Muriel and Savary, Louis M. The Heart of Friendship. New York: Harper & Row, 1976.

   An interpretation of the development, practice, stresses, importance, and transactions of friendship, with extensive literary references, from Transactional Analysis and self-actualizing psychological points of view.

144. Johnson, D. W. and Johnson, F. P. Joining Together: Group Theory and Group Skills. Englewood Cliffs, N.J.: Prentice-Hall, 1975.

145. Jourard, Sidney M. The Transparent Self. New York: D. Van Nostrand, 1975.

   An exploration of the importance of self-disclosure in all relationships, especially marriage, therapy, and friendship. See especially pages 17 and 53 on friendship as well as Jourard's view that males lack insight and empathy, necessary qualities for an open relationship like friendship (pages 34-41).

146. Journal of Social and Personal Relationships. London: Sage. Quarterly, beginning with Volume 1, Number 1, March 1984. Steve Duck, Editor.

   An interdisciplinary journal (psychology, sociology, communications) concerned with personal relationships, especially friendship and romance. Pertinent articles in this first volume include: D. P. McAdams and M. Losoff, "Friendship Motivation in Fourth and Sixth Graders: A Thematic Analysis"; R. B. Hays, "The Development and Maintenance of Friendship"; and P. H. Wright, "Self-reference Motivation and the Intrinsic Quality of Friendship."

147. Journal of Social and Personal Relationships. London: Sage, June 1984. (Volume 1, Number 2)

   See especially Michael Argyle and Monika Henderson,

"The Rules of Friendship" and Pat O'Connor and George W. Brown, "Supportive Relationships: Fact or Fancy?", about the very close relationships of a sample of 60 married women, between the ages of 20 and 42, living in London.

148. Journal of Social and Personal Relationships. London: Sage, September 1984. (Volume 1, Number 3)

Includes the following friendship-related articles: Suzanna M. Rose, "How Friendships End: Patterns Among Young Adults"; Harriet Sants, "Conceptions of Friendship, Social Behaviour and School Achievement in Six-Year-Old Children"; and Lenahan O'Connell, "An Exploration of Exchange in Three Social Relationships: Kinship, Friendship and the Marketplace."

149. Journal of Social and Personal Relationships. London: Sage, December 1984. (Volume 1, Number 4) (in press)

Articles to be included are, among others: Virginia Blankenship, Steven M. Knat, Thomas G. Hess, and Donald R. Brown, "Reciprocal Interaction and Similarity of Personality Attributes" and David D. Clarke, Christine M.B. Allen and Sara Dickson, "The Characteristic Affective Tone of Seven Classes of Interpersonal Relationship."

150. Journal of Social and Personal Relationships. London: Sage, March 1985. (Volume 2, Number 1) (in preparation)

Planned articles include "The Coming Revolution in Human Relationships."

151. Kadushin, Charles. Why People Go To Psychiatrists. New York: Atherton, 1969.

Sociologist Kadushin, a leading authority on social networks, discusses the importance of friends (and having a friend who is already seeing a psychiatrist) in determining whether or not someone seeks psychiatric help.

152. Kant, Immanuel. "Friendship" in Lecture on Ethics.
Translated by Louis Infield. New York: Harper Torchbooks,
1963.

153. Kanter, Rosabeth Moss. Men and Women of the Corporation.
New York: Basic Books, 1977.

   Sociologist Kanter discusses the friendships of the
wives of managers (pages 116-117, 119) as well as gossip,
social isolation, and power at Indsco, the pseudonym for the
corporation that she studied for this classic exploration of
working in a corporation.

154. Karweit, Nancy Lynne. "Student Friendship Networks as a
Resource Within Schools." Unpublished Ph.D. thesis, Johns
Hopkins University, 1976.

155. Kaufman, Debra Renee. "Social Network Analysis of
Colleague Friend Relationships in Academia: Male and Female
Differences." Unpublished Ph.D. thesis, Cornell University,
1975.

156. Kelley, Eleanor Ann. "Peer Group Friendships in One Class
of High School Girls: Change and Stability." Unpublished
Ph.D. thesis, Michigan State University, 1966.

157. Kelley, H.H.; Berscheid, E.; Christensen, A.; Harvey, J.;
Huston, T.; Levinger, G.; McClintock, E.; Peplau, A.; and
Peterson, D., eds. Close Relationships. San Francisco:
Freeman, 1982.

158. Kennedy, Eugene. On Being a Friend. New York:
Ballantine Books, 1982.

   A general book by a psychologist, and a former priest,
who is also the author of The Joy of Being Human.

159. Knapp, Mark L. Social Intercourse: From Greeting to
Goodbye. Boston: Allyn and Bacon, Inc., 1978.

160. Komarovsky, Mirra. Blue Collar Marriage. New York:
Vintage Books, 1967.

161. Kornblum, William. <u>Blue Collar Community.</u> Chicago: University of Chicago Press, 1974.

    Sociologist Kornblum's intensive community study of South Chicago. Discusses friendship as a primary group in adolescence and as a factor in work and community life.

162. Krantzler, Mel. <u>Creative Divorce.</u> New York: New American Library, 1973.

163. La Rochefoucauld, Francois de. <u>The Maxims of La Rochefoucauld.</u> Translated by Louis Kronenberger. New York: Random House, 1959.

164. Lang, Olga. <u>Chinese Family and Society.</u> New Haven, CT: Yale University Press, 1946.

    Includes a chapter on friendship, Confucian views on the subject, and a friend as confident for youth in modern China.

165. Lasch, Christopher. <u>The Culture of Narcissism: American Life in an Age of Diminishing Expectations.</u> New York: Norton, 1979.

166. _____. <u>Haven in a Heartless World: The Family Besieged.</u> New York: Basic Books, 1977.

    See "Friendship, the New 'Religion,'" pages 100-106.

167. Leefeldt, Christine and Callenbach, Ernest. <u>The Art of Friendship.</u> New York: Berkley Books, 1980.

    A book for a general audience that discusses men and women friendships, friendship and marriage, resolving conflicts in friendship, and creative friendship.

168. Lepp, Ignace. <u>The Ways of Friendship: A Psychological Exploration of Man's Most Valuable Relationships.</u> New York: Macmillan, 1966.

169. Levinson, Daniel J. with Darrow, Charlotte N.; Klein, Edward B.; Levinson, Maria H; and McKee, Braxton. The Seasons of a Man's Life. New York: Ballantine Books, 1978.

A lack of close friendships was reported by the middle-aged males that Levinson and his associates studied.

170. Lewis, Michael and Rosenblum, Leonard A., eds. Friendship and Peer Relations. New York: Wiley, 1975.

An overview of research till 1975 on infant and toddler peer relations.

171. Leyton, Elliot, ed. The Compact: Selected Dimensions of Friendship. Newfoundland Social and Economic Papers, No. 3, Institute of Social and Economic Research, Memorial University of Newfoundland. Toronto: University of Toronto Press, 1974.

Includes Cora DuBois' "The Gratuitous Act: An Introduction to the Comparative Study of Friendship Patterns."

172. Liebow, Elliot. Tally's Corner: A Study of Negro Streetcorner Men. Introduction by Hylan Lewis. Boston: Little, Brown, 1967.

Anthropologist Liebow's well-written account of a group of adult black males who, during the early 1960s, hung out together on a corner of Washington D.C.'s inner city. Includes a chapter dealing with "Friends and Networks." Liebow notes the unique role that friendship plays in the lives of his streetcorner men: "It is as if friendship is an artifact of desire, a wish relationship, a private agreement between two people to act 'as if,' rather than a real relationship between persons."

173. Lindsey, Karen. Friends as Family. Boston: Beacon Press, 1981.

The theme of Lindsey's popular book is revealed in these words: "...even in the face of a society that tells us friends are friends and family is family and never the twain shall meet, many of us unconsciously choose friends to be part of, or even all of, our family."

174. Lipnack, Jessica and Stamps, Jeffrey. Networking: The First Report and Directory. Garden City, N. Y.: Doubleday, 1982.

175. Lively, Penelope. Perfect Happiness. Garden City, N.Y.: Dial/Doubleday, 1984. (Fiction)

The story of best friends who became sisters-in-law. The August 24, 1984 Publishers Weekly review praises the book in this way: "Their story is as rich and twisted and surprising as life; it is indeed life, raised to a pitch of drama and intensity that the author's wit, elegance and sensitivity sustain and continuously sharpen."

176. Lopata, Helena Znaniecka. Occupation: Housewife. New York: Oxford University Press, 1971.

177. _____. Women as Widows: Support Systems. New York: Elsevier North-Holland, 1979.

An extensive study of a sample of over 1,000 Chicago area widows including a detailed chapter on friends. Lopata suggests a typology of friendships for the widows that she studied: the friendless widow; the casually interactive widow; the polite companionship widow; and the widow in multifaceted friendships.

178. _____ and Maines, David, eds. Research in the Interweave of Social Roles: Friendship, A Research Annual. Vol. 2. Greenwich, CT: JAI Press, 1981.

Included are the following articles: H. Lopata, "Friendship: Historical and Theoretical Introduction"; B. Brown, "A life-span Approach to Friendship: Age-related Dimensions of an Ageless Relationship"; M. Suelzle, "The Structuring of Friendship Formation Among Two-to-five-year-old Children Enrolled in Full Day Care"; J. Acker, K. Barry, and J. Esseveld, "Feminism, Female Friends and the Reconstruction of Intimacy"; E. Bankoff, "Effects of Friendship Support on the Psychological Well-being of Widows"; J. Levy, "Friendship Dilemmas and the Interaction of Social Worlds: Re-entry Women on the College Campus"; D. Maines, "The Organizational and Career Contexts of Friendship Among Postdoctoral Researchers"; T. Gannon, "Friendship Patterns of the American Catholic Clergy"; R. Little, "Friendships in the Military Community"; J. Gustfield, J. Kotarba, and P. Rasmussen, "The Public Society of Intimates: Friends, Wives, Lovers and Others in Drinking-Driving Drama"; and W. Baker and R. Hertz, "Communal Diffusion of Friendship: The Structure of Intimate Relations in an Israeli Kibbutz."

179. Lynch, James J. The Broken Heart: The Medical Consequences of Loneliness. New York: Basic Books, 1977.

A powerful book, reinforced with statistics and references, stressing the medical (not just the emotional), ill-effects if the need for intimate companionship is unmet. Although the emphasis is on romantic and family attachments, friendship is discussed in chapter 8, "Denying the Problem: Loneliness Traps."

180. Lynd, Robert S. and Lynd, Helen Merrell. Middletown: A Study in Modern American Culture. New York: Harcourt, Brace & World, 1929, 1956.

See the chapter on "The Organization of Leisure," especially pages 272-6, for a discussion of the friendships of the residents of Middletown in the early 1900s.

181. Machlowitz, Marilyn. Workaholics. Reading, MA: Addison-Wesley, 1980.

Psychologist Machlowitz found that, for the workaholics she studied, friendship was less important to them than their work and, as a possible consequence of that attitude, friendships were sometimes maintained as a way of advancing their careers.

182. Malinowski, Bronislaw. Crime and Custom in Savage Society. London: Routledge & Kegan Paul, 1926; reprint ed.,

Totowa, N.J.: Littlefield, Adams, 1972.

183. Marty, Martin E. Friendship. Niles, IL: Argus Communications, 1980.

184. Maslow, Abraham H. Motivation and Personality. Second edition. New York: Harper & Row, 1954, 1970.

   See pages 44 and 249-53 on the "shallowness of American friendship" and good friendships as a paradigm of effective interpersonal relations.

185. Masterson, George. "Friendship as a Situational Phenomenon: A Study of Friendship Among College Freshmen." Unpublished Ph.D. thesis, University of Pittsburgh, 1956.

186. Mauss, Marcel. The Gift. New York: Norton, 1967.

   A classic social anthopological discussion of reciprocity and the exchange of gifts.

187. May, Rollo. Love and Will. New York: Norton, 1969.

188. McCall, George J. and Simmons, J. L. Identities and Interactions. Second edition. New York: Free Press, 1966, 1978.

   Sociologists McCall and Simmons, basing their discussion on Simmel's insights about the dyad, note that it is intimacy, the strength of a genuine friendship, that can also be the source of its extinction. Intimates see behaviors not shown to others; by only showing the intimate side, the friendship pair come to get a myopic view of each other. "The relationship itself thus becomes trivial and unsatisfying," McCall and Simmons note, and intimacy can also lead to jealousy -- the knowledge of, or fear that, intimacies are being shared with someone other than the intimate.

189. McCall, George J.; McCall, Michal M.; Denzin, Norman K.; Suttles, Gerald D.; and Kurth, Suzanne B. Social Relationships. Chicago: Aldine, 1970.

All five authors of this insightful collection of scholarly articles on friendship had been associated with each other at the Urbana campus of the University of Illinois during the 1960s; they all had "exposure to the symbolic interactionist tradition." In Suttles' frequently-cited essay, "Friendship as a Social Institution," how friendship as a social institution "fits into the general pattern of total societies and fulfills certain social functions" is dealt with. What is the function of friendship? According to Suttles, friendship "...fills in where the more mechanical and exclusionary institutions fail to define interpersonal affiliations." Friendship also has three defining elements: it is a "very generalized relationship and can occur within strata or existing groups as well as between them; it is "a voluntaristic and intensely personal relation"; and "friendships are subject to private negotiation to an extent unparalleled in most other social relations."

Suttles' main theme is that true friendship is based upon the presentation of one's "real self" to another. It is the ability to disregard the "rules of public propriety" that individuals must generally live by that distinguishes friendship from other institutional relationships. Suttles sees one of the reasons that friendships are maintained is that, acting in a deviant manner with each other, friends may have information that they could use to harm each other and thus "...a sort of mutual blackmail may force their relation forward despite a lack of gratification on the part of one member." A fundamental problem with Suttles' view of friendship is his notion that friendship fosters the revelation of a "true" of "deviant" self, as if friendship might not show to that "alter" (other) only one side perhaps as limited or as another side presented in, for instance, a business setting. Thus, it can be as unfriendly to talk shop at length with friends as it may be unprofessional to talk about personal matters with most business associates.

In Kurth's essay, "Friendship and Friendly Relations," a clear distinction is made between friendship and friendly relations, the former being a relationship that is not easily ended; the latter being a relationship into which one can quite easily drift in and out. Friendly relations are usually tied to a formal role and/or external event. Thus a friendship should be less altered by external changes since a "friendship requires that one build a substantial relationship on other bases, so that it will persist even if the formal role relationship is dissolved."

190. McGinnis, Alan Loy. The Friendship Factor: How to Get Closer to the People You Care For. Minneapolis: Augsburg, 1979.

   A popular self-help book by McGinnis, a pastor and counselor, covering such aspects of friendship as self-disclosure, conversational skills, loyalty, forgiveness, and ways of salvaging a faltering one.

191. Mead, Margaret. Blackberry Winter: My Earlier Years. New York: Morrow, 1972.

192. _____. Coming of Age in Samoa. New York: William Morrow and Company, 1939.

193. _____ and Wolfenstein, Martha. Childhood in Contemporary Cultures. Chicago: University of Chicago Pres, 1955.

   Includes references to friendship in Asian and European communities, from the perspective of anthropologists.

194. Meilaender, Gilbert C. Friendship: A Study in Theological Ethics. Notre Dame, IN: University of Notre Dame Press, 1981.

195. Merrill, Susan Lee. "Patterns and Functions of Close Friendship in Relation to Personal Adjustment." Unpublished Ph.,D. thesis, University of Minnesota, 1974.

196. Mettetal, Gwendolyn. "The Conversations of Female Friends at Three Ages: The Importance of Fantasy, Gossip, and Self-disclosure." Unpublished Ph.D. thesis, University of Illinois, 1982.

197. Michaelis, David. The Best of Friends: Profiles of Extraordinary Friendships. New York: Morrow, 1983.

198. Michaels, Leonard. The Men's Club. New York: Farrar Straus Giroux, 1981. (Fiction)

Seven men meet one night in Berkeley, California to form a friendship group. "Friendship is a luxury," says a reluctant joiner. "Unless you're so poor it makes no difference how you spend your time."

199. Miller, Charles H. <u>Auden: An American Friendship</u>. New York: Scribner's, 1983.

200. Miller, Stuart. <u>Men & Friendship</u>. Boston: Houghton Mifflin, 1983.

   Miller, a former director of the Esalen Institute, reports on the dearth of intimate friendship among contemporary Western men. Some of the reasons for this, according to Miller, are as follows: "The fear of homosexuality and how it affects the possibilities of male friendship in our times are topics that need contemplating...the estate of male friendship -- indeed, of nearly all human relationships -- is sufficiently sunk that mere sex remains at the center of people's imaginations. The only moving human relationships that people seem able to conjure up are erotic ones."

201. Mills, Laurens Joseph. <u>One Soul in Bodies Twain: Friendship in Tudor Literature and Stuart Drama</u>. Bloomington, IN: Principia Press, 1937.

202. Mitchell, James Clyde. <u>Social Networks in Urban Situations</u>. Manchester: Manchester University Press, 1969.

203. Moustakis, Clark. <u>Loneliness</u>. Englewood Cliffs, N.J.: Prentice-Hall, 1961.

204. Murstein, Bernard I., ed. <u>Exploring Intimate Life Styles</u>. New York: Springer, 1978.

205. Neuwirth, Gertrud R. "Friendship Patterns and Organizational Participation: A Study in Ambience." Unpublished Ph.D. thesis, University of Minnesota, 1959.

206. Newcomb, Theodore M. <u>The Acquaintance Process</u>. New York: Holt, Rinehart and Winston, 1961.

207. Newman, Mildred and Berkowitz, Bernard. How to Be Your Own Best Friend. London: Pan Books, 1974.

208. Nietzsche, Friedrich. Beyond Good and Evil. Translated with commentary by Walter Kaufmann. New York: Vintage Books, 1966.

   On friends and friendship, see TP, 27, 40, 195, 217, 260, 268, and 283.

209. _____. The Gay Science. Translated with commentary by Walter Kaufmann. New York: Vintage Books, 1974.

   On friendship, see T12, 14, 16, 61, 279, 279n, 329, 364, 366, J14, and J25.

210. Nisbet, Robert A. The Sociological Tradition. New York: Basic Books, Inc., Publishers, 1966.

211. Norton, David L. and Kille, Mary F., editors. Philosophies of Love. Totowa, N.J.: Rowman & Allanheld, Publishers, 1983.

   See especially Part 5, "Friendship," which includes excerpts from pertinent writings by Aristotle, Plato, Emerson, Schopenhauer, and Buber.

212. Oakes, Thomas Warren. "Primary Group Relations in Sick Role Behavior: Perceived Family and Friends' Expectations in Patient Compliance." Unpublished Ph.D. thesis, University of Utah, 1970.

213. Oden, Sherri Lee. "Coaching Children in Social Skills for Friendship-Making." Unpublished Ph.D. thesis, University of Illinois at Urbana-Champaign, 1975.

214. Olmsted, Michael S. and Hare, A. Paul. The Small Group, 2nd ed. New York: Random House, 1978.

215. Osofsky, Joy D., ed. Handbook of Infant Development. New York: Wiley, 1980.

Contains a comprehensive review of research on early peer relations.

216. O'Shea, Robert Michael. "Homophily and Friendship Choice in Dental School." Unpublished Ph.D. thesis, Catholic University of America, 1965.

217. Parsons, Talcott. The Social System. New York: Free Press, 1951.

218. _____ and Shils, Edward A., eds. Toward a General Theory of Action. Cambridge: Harvard University Press, 1951.

   See Samuel A. Stouffer and Jackson Toby, "Role Conflict and Personality," for a discussion of the conflicts in "one's institutionalized obligations of friendship and one's institutionalized obligations to a society."

219. Peplau, Letitia Anne and Perlman, Dan, eds. Loneliness: A Sourcebook of Current Research, Theory and Therapy. New York: Wiley-Interscience, 1982.

220. Petersen, Elwnoe Langston. "Some Role Dimensions of Loyalty: A Study of Obligations and Privileges Associated with Attitudes of Loyalty Toward Parents, Friend, and Country." Unpublished Ph.D. thesis, University of California, Los Angeles, 1963.

221. Phillips, Gerald M. and Wood, Julia T. Communication and Human Relationships: The Study of Interpersonal Communication. New York: Macmillan, 1983.

   See chapter 9, "The Men Testify," and chapter 10, "The Women Testify," for male and female views on friendship, based on the authors' analyses of a written friendship survey of over 1,000 respondents (a majority were college students).

222. Plato, Lysis, or Friendship in The Works of Plato, selected and edited by Irwin Edman. Based on the standard,

authorized text of the Jowett translation. New York: Modern Library, 1928, pp. 3-32.

    Although <u>Lysis</u> is Plato's central work on friendship, it is a theme that is also touched on in his other works, such as the <u>Symposium, Phaedrus, Timaeus, Republic, Statesman,</u> and <u>Laws</u>. <u>Lysis</u>, a dialogue about friendship, has Socrates as the narrator and Hippothales, Menexenus, Lysis, and Ctesippus as the participants. Through the friendship of two boys, Lysis and Menexenus, <u>Lysis</u> explores the concept of friendship. It examines the contradictions behind such general ideas about friendship, such as: if one is wise and good, and therefore useful to others, one will have friends, yet the "ultimate principle of friendship is not for the sake of any other or further dear"; or "friends have all things in common," yet unequals seek each other out for friendship. The dialogue concludes, however, without resolving these conradictions.

223. _____. <u>The Republic</u>. Translated by B. Jowett. New York: Modern Library, 1941.

224. Pleck, Joseph and Sawyer, Jack. <u>Men and Masculinity</u>. Englewood Cliffs, N.J.: Prentice-Hall, 1974.

    See the section called "Men and Men."

225. Plutarch. <u>On Love, The Family, and the Good Life: Selected Essays of Plutarch</u>. Translated by Moses Hadas. New York: New American Library, 1957.

    See "Dialogue on Love," "On Brotherly Love," "Marriage Counsel," and "How One May Distinguish Between Flatterer and Friend."

226. Price, Richard. <u>Ladies' Man</u>. Boston: Houghton Mifflin, 1978. (<u>Fiction</u>)

227. Reisman, John M. <u>Anatomy of Friendship</u>. New York: Irvington, 1979.

228. Reohr, J. "The Place of Reciprocity in Friendship."

Unpublished Ph.D. thesis, Boston University, 1978.

229. Riesman, David with Glazer, Nathan and Denney, Reuel. <u>The Lonely Crowd: A Study of the Changing American Character</u>. Abridged ed. New Haven: Yale University Press, 1961.

    The classic study of "inner-direction" and "outer-direction" as examples of "social character."

230. Rolon, Michael E. <u>Interpersonal Communication: The Social Exchange Approach</u>. Beverly Hills: Sage, 1981.

231. Rooney, James Francis. "Friendship and Reference Group Orientation Among Skid Row Men." Unpublished Ph.D. thesis, University of Pennsylvania, 1973.

232. Rosow, Irving. <u>Socialization to Old Age</u>. Berkeley: University of California Press, 1974.

    This book "on adult socialization theory" contains a chapter on peer group functions.

233. Rossi, Peter H. <u>Why Families Move</u>. Glencoe, IL: Free Press, 1955.

    Sociologist Rossi's empirical study of urban mobility includes a discussion of the relationship between friendship patterns, socioeconomic status, and residential mobility.

234. Rubin, Lillian Breslow. <u>Intimate Strangers: Men and Women Together</u>. New York: Harper & Row, 1983.

    Rubin, a psychotherapist, suggests that early gender role training is responsible for the disparate ways of relating that men and women must cope with later on in their intimate relationships. On friendship, see pages 129-32.

235. _____. <u>Worlds of Pain: Life in the Working-Class Family</u>. New York: Basic Books, 1976.

    Based on intensive interviews, this is a memorable

study, illustrated with direct quotations, of the differences in marital and friendship patterns between lower- and upper middle-class couples.

236. Rubin, Zick. Children's Friendships. (The Developing Child Series) Cambridge: Harvard University Press, 1980.

A well-written, descriptive summary, based on social psychologist Rubin's observations and literature research of the development and importance of friendship from the earliest months of life. Rubin, who also teaches a college course on friendship, includes practical suggestions in his book, such as how children may become friends, skills for friendship maintenance, and coping with friendship dissolution.

237. _____. Liking and Loving: An Invitation to Social Psychology. New York: Holt, Rinehart and Winston, 1973.

238. Rysman, Alexander Romm. "Friendship and Authority: Specific and Diffuse Relations in a Hospital Hierarchy." Unpublished Ph.D. thesis, New York University, 1972.

239. Sarma, Jyotirmoyee. "The Social Categories of Friendship." Unpublished Ph.D. thesis, University of Chicago, 1946.

240. Schofield, William. Psychotherapy: The Purchase of Friendship. Englewood Cliffs, N.J.: Prentice-Hall, 1964.

241. Schopenhauer. The Philosophy of Schopenhauer. Edited, with an introduction, by Irwin Edman. New York: Modern Library, 1928, 1956.

242. Schur, E. M. The Awareness Trap: Self-absorption Instead of Social Change. New York: Quadrangle Books, 1977.

243. Sebald, Hans. Adolescence: A Social Psychological Analysis. Second edition. Englewood Cliffs, N.J.: Prentice-Hall, 1968, 1977.

In his textbook on adolescence, Sebald cites these four major values of teenagers: friendship, popularity (as distinct from friendship), prestige, and sex.

244. Selden, Elizabeth S. The Book of Friendship: An International Anthology. Boston: Houghton Mifflin, 1947.

245. Selman, Robert L. The Growth of Interpersonal Understanding: Developmental and Clinical Analyses. New York: Academic Press, 1980.

246. Seneca, Gail. "Marital Interaction and Friendship Networks." Unpublished Ph.D. thesis, New York University, 1979.

247. Shain, Merle. Some Men Are More Perfect Than Others. New York: Bantam Books, 1974.

248. _____. When Lovers are Friends. New York: Bantam Books, 1978.

249. Sheehy, Gail. Passages: Predictable Crises of Adult Life. New York: Bantam Books, 1977.

A journalist's best seller about the crises, and phases, men and women go through from eighteen to fifty. See pages 85-7 on deviant peer groups.

250. Shuval, Judith T. "Class and Ethnicity: A Study in Social Structure and Interpersonal Relations." Unpublished Ph.D. thesis, Radcliffe College, 1955.

251. Simmel, Georg. Conflict & The Web of Group-Affiliations. Translated by Kurt H. Wolff and Reinhard Bendix. Foreword by Everett C. Hughes. New York: Free Press, 1955.

Simmel's 1904 essay details the "sociologically positive character of conflict." Not only does Simmel see conflict as resolving "the tension between contrasts" but as an expression of genuine intimacy. Simmel also notes that conflict may be expressed indirectly in competition; it may also be the basis of group formation.

252. _____. The Sociology of George Simmel. Translated and

edited by Kurt H. Wolff. New York: Free Press, 1950.

Simmel's fundamental writings on the nature of the dyad and the triad ("The Isolated Individual and the Dyad" and "The Triad") are related to friendship (and love relations). A dyad is more intimate, but less stable since it takes only one member to end it. A triad is less intimate, but the third person "serves the perpetuation of the group." Simmel points out that "No matter how close a triad may be, there is always the occasion on which two of the three members regard the third as an intruder." Contemporary communications analysts, such as Wilmot, refer to this as a "dyadic coalition."
In "Friendship and Love" in the chapter, "Types of Social Relationships by Degrees of Reciprocal Knowledge of Their Participants," Simmel discusses his concept of differentiated friendship, namely friendships "which cover only one side of the personality, without playing into other aspects of it." Simmel, typifying ideal friendships of antiquity as those with "...absolute psychological intimacy..." where "even material property should be common...," states: "Modern man, possibly, has too much to hide to sustain a friendship in the ancient sense." According to Simmel, having numerous differentiated friends, each sharing something but not everything, may be the kind of friendship more compatible with modern society.

253. Slater, Philip E. The Pursuit of Loneliness. Boston: Beacon Press, 1970.

   Includes a discussion of friendship in American culture.

254. Smiley, Jane. Duplicate Keys. New York: Knopf, 1984. (Fiction)

   In her review in the New York Times Book Review (April 29, 1984), novelist Lois Gould writes: "This may be the anatomy of a murder... More important and far more compelling is the anatomy of friendship, betrayal..."

255. Smucker, Orden C. "A Sociographic Study of the Friendship Patterns on a College Campus." Unpublished Ph.D. thesis,

Ohio State University, 1946.

256. Srole, Leo, et al. Mental Health in the Metropolis: The Midtown Manhattan Study. New York: McGraw-Hill, 1962.

257. Sparks, James Allen. Friendship After Forty. Nashville, TN: Abingdon, 1980.

258. Stein, Peter J. Single. Englewood Cliffs, N.J.: Prentice-Hall, 1976.

   In sociologist Stein's study of singles -- based on two samples of younger (college-age) and older (25 to 45) singles -- friendship was found to be very important, especially among the Older Sample. "Friendship, clearly, played an important part in the lives of the Sample B single people we interviewed. They did not in any sense seem to conform to the old stereotype of lonely singles." Sources of friendship included memberships in a variety of men's and women's groups, same-sex friends, and past opposite-sex romantic partners who were now friends.

259. _____, ed. Single Life: Unmarried Adults in Social Context. New York: St. Martin's Press, 1981.

   Includes Beth B. Hess' chapter, "Friendship and Gender Roles over the Life Course" and Robert S. Weiss' "The Study of Loneliness."

260. Stocking, S. Holly; Arezzo, Diana; and Leavitt, Shelley. Helping Kids Make Friends. Allen, TX: Argus Communications, 1979. (In cooperation with The Boys Town Center for the Study of Youth Development.)

261. Strong, Leslie Dale. "The Intimate Friendship Network and Group Marriage: An Empirical Investigation of Contemporary InterFamily Cooperation." Unpublished Ph.D. thesis, Florida State University, 1975.

262. Sullivan, Harry Stack. The Interpersonal Theory of Psychiatry. New York: Norton, 1953.

   Psychologist Sullivan states his belief that children

are incapable of being real friends until the ages of eight to ten. Sullivan distinguishes the juvenile years as ones marked by the need for playmates and the preadolescent years (about ages seven through twelve) by "the development of the need for peers, for playmates rather like oneself," including finding a close friend or chum.

263. Taylor, Jeremy. A Discourse on Friendship. Cedar Rapids, IA: Torch Press, 1913.

264. Tennov, Dorothy. Love and Limerance: The Experience of Being in Love. New York: Stein and Day, 1979.

    Psychologist Tennov shares her observation that true love only begins after three years of limerance.

265. Thoreau, Henry. The Portable Thoreau. Edited by Carl Bode. Revised edition. New York: Viking Press, 1947, 1964.

    On friendship, see A Week on the Concord and Merrimack Rivers, Walden, and "Great Friend," a poem.

266. Tiger, Lionel. Men in Groups. New York: Random House, 1969.

    "Male bonding" is the term Tiger used to describe man's need for male camaraderie.

267. Todd, Janet M. Women's Friendship in Literature. New York: Columbia University Press, 1980.

268. Tonnies, Ferdinand. Community & Society (Gemeinfchaft und Gesellschaft. Translated and edited by Charles P. Loomis. New York: Harper & Row, (1887), 1963.

269. Troyat, Henri. An Intimate Friendship. Trans. from French by Joyce Emerson. London: Redman, 1967.

270. Tschann, Jeanne M. "Adult Friendship: Effects of Gender and Life-stage on Closeness, Meaning of Friendship and Patterns of Socializing." Unpublished Ph.D. thesis, Unversity of California, Santa Cruz, 1983.

271. Useem, Michael. "Involvement in a Radical Political Movement and Patterns of Friendship: The Draft Resistance Community." Unpublished Ph.D. thesis, Harvard University, 1970.

272. Vaillant, George E. Adaptation to Life. Boston: Little, Brown, 1977.

273. Van Gennep, Arnold. The Rites of Passage. Translated by Monika B. Vizedom and Gabrielle L. Caffee. Chicago: University of Chicago Press, 1960.

274. Verbrugge, Lois Marie. "Adult Friendship Contact: Time Constraints and Status-Homogeneity Effects, Detroit and Juelich, West Germany." Unpublished Ph.D. thesis, University of Michigan, 1974.

275. Wallach, Anne Tolstoi. Women's Work. New York: New American Library, 1981. (Fiction)

   In this well-written but highly stereotyped account of a divorced woman executive with two grown children trying to make it in the advertising world, the heroine does have a best friend. Interestingly enough, however, she only "gets her man" after the best friend dies suddenly, the victim of heart failure while undergoing face lift surgery, as if one cannot have both "a man" and "a best girlfriend."

276. Walster, Elaine, and Walster, G. William. A New Look at Love. Reading, MA: Addison-Wesley, 1978.

277. Weber, Max. Economy and Society: An Outline of Interpretive Sociology. Vols. 1 & 2. Edited by Guenther Roth and Claus Wittich. Translated by Ephraim Fischoff, Hans Gerth, A. M. Henderson, Ferdinand Kolegar, C. Wright Mills, Talcott Parsons, Max Rheinstein, Guenther Roth, Edward Shils, and Claus Wittich. Berkeley: University of California Press, 1978.

278. _____. The Theory of Social and Economic Organization. Translated by A.M. Henderson and T. Parsons. New York: Oxford University Press, 1947.

279. Weiss, Robert S., ed. Loneliness: The Experience of Emotional and Social Isolation. Foreword by David Riesman. Cambridge: MIT Press, 1973.

280. Weiss, Robert S. Marital Separation. New York: Basic Books, 1975.

   Based on the Seminars for the Separated which sociologist Weiss conducted, this informative and helpful book has a chapter on "Friends: The Changes in Relationships With Them" as well as discussions of forming new post-separation friendships.

281. Whyte, William Foote. Street Corner Society: The Social Structure of an Italian Slum. 2nd ed. Chicago: University of Chicago Press, 1955.

282. _____. The Organization Man. New York: Simon and Schuster, 1956.

   See pages 330-61, "The Web of Friendship."

283. Williams, James Howard. "Primary Friendship Relations of Housewives in Two Social Status Areas: Columbia, South Carolina." Unpublished Ph.D. thesis, Vanderbilt University, 1956.

284. Wilmot, William W. Dyadic Communication. Second edition. Reading, MA: Addison-Wesley, 1979, 1975.

285. Wood, Margaret M. The Stranger: A Study in Social Relationships. New York: Columbia University Press, 1934.

286. Woods, Ralph L., ed. A Treasury of Friendship. New York: McKay, 1957.

   Includes Rousseau's "Jean Jacques Rousseau Gives Madame D'Epinay His Rules For Friendship" and Jacques Barzun's "The Teacher in America," about friendship and pedagogy.

287. Young, Michael and Willmott, Peter. Family and Kinship in East London. Rev. ed. Baltimore: Penguin Books, 1962.

288. Zewe, Martin Donald. "Family, Friends, and Religious Attitudes: A Study of Communality Among Suburban Catholics." Unpublished Ph.D. Thesis, Columbia University, 1974.

289. Zimbardo, Philip G. *Shyness*. Reading, MA: Addison-Wesley, 1977.

ARTICLES (AND CHAPTERS) IN JOURNALS, BOOKS,
ENCYCLOPEDIAS, MAGAZINES, AND NEWSPAPERS

290. Adams, Bert N. "Isolation, Function and Beyond: American Kinship in the 1960's." *Journal of Marriage and the Family* 32 (November 1970):575-97.

291. _____. "The Middle-Class Adult and His Widowed or Still-married Mother." *Social Problems* 16 (1968):50-9.

292. Adams, Jane. "Hers." *New York Times*, September 18, 1980, p. C2.

   A column about the friends who come to stay in Adams' spare room as they sort out their romantic lives. Adams is amazed at the endurance of her friendships, as well as her parents' 45-year-marriage, compared to the seeming transience of her friends' marriages.

293. Adams, Margaret. "The Single Woman in Today's Society: A Reappraisal." *American Journal of Orthopsychiatry* 41 (October 1971):776-86.

   In one of the best early serious articles on single women, Adams discusses their friendships, noting some of the problems that they face, including using girlfriends "as a stopgap to ward off loneliness and fill the time, pending a more rewarding relationship with a man" and the dilemma of the "friendly threesome" in trying to maintain friendships with girlfriends who have married.

294. Albrecht, Stan L. "Reactions and Adjustments to Divorce: Differences in the Experiences of Males and Females." *Family Relations* 29 (January 1980):59-68.

   Sociologist Albrecht compares the divorce experiences

of males and females for a sample of 500 divorced persons from eight Rocky Mountain states. Several questions were asked to determine the impact of divorce on friendship patterns and social interaction. For this sample, withdrawal and self-imposed isolation were infrequent responses to divorce. Almost twice as many respondents reported an increase in participation in organizations and clubs rather than a decrease in such activities. Female respondents reported more post-divorce involvement with their relatives than did males.

295. Alger, William Rounsville. "The Literature of Friendship." North American Review 172 (July 1856):104-32.

296. Allan, Graham. "Class Variation in Friendship Patterns." British Journal of Sociology 28 (September 1977):389-93.

    Based on interviews with twenty-one middle-class and twenty working class respondents in a largely suburban Essex, England, village, sociologist Allan looks at systematic differences in the way these respondents organize their non-kin social relationships. Allan's major finding is that working class couples confine their non-kin social relationship "to particular situations" whereas middle-class couples "'flowered out' to include other types of activity." Furthermore, the working class respondents regarded fewer persons as friends.

297. _____. "Sibling Solidarity." Journal of Marriage and the Family 39 (1977):177-84.

298. Allon, Natalie and Fishel, Diane. "Singles' Bars as Examples of Urban Courting Patterns." In Single Life, pp. 115-28. Edited by P. J. Stein. New York: St. Martin's Press, Inc., 1981.

299. Anderson, Jane. "Challenges and Rewards of Living Single". Christian Science Monitor, January 20, 1983, p. 15.

300. Argyle, Michael and Henderson, Monika. "The Rules of Friendship." Journal of Social and Personal Relationships 1 (June 1984):211-37.

The authors summarize the findings of their four studies on the rules of friendship. Four rules were "highly endorsed across all four cultures" in their British, Italian, Hong Kong, and Japanese samples. Those rules are: respecting each other's privacy; trusting and confiding in each other; volunteering to help in time of need; and not being jealous or critical of each other's relationships.

301. Arling, Greg. "The Elderly Widow and Her Family, Neighbors and Friends." Journal of Marriage and the Family 38 (November 1976):757-68.

    This is a comparison of the involvement of 409 elderly widows with family and friendship/neighboring. Arling found that friendship-neighboring was related to less loneliness and worry; contact with family members, particularly children, did not elevate morale.

302. _____. "Resistance to Isolation Among Elderly Widows." International Journal of Aging and Human Development 7 (1976a):67-86.

303. Asher, Steven R. and Hymel, Shelley. "Children's Social Competence in Peer Relations: Sociometric and Behavioral Assessment", Chapter 5, pp. 128-57. In Social Competence, edited by J.D. Wine and M.D. Smye. New York: Guilford Press, 1981.

304. Ashton, E.T. "Friendship and Mental Health." Mental Health 13 (1953):5-8.

305. Babchuk, Nicholas. "Primary Friends and Kin: A Study of the Association of Middle Class Couples." Social Forces 43 (1965):483-93.

    Following up his previous study (with Bates) on the friendship patterns of middle class couples, Babchuk confirmed their original findings: that husbands initiated, and determined, mutual friendships more often than their wives. Babchuk also discovered that frequent association with relatives did not predict the pattern for visits with friends. About half the wives and husbands in his study did not have even one primary friend independent of their spouse; the modal number of local primary friend units in the second study was two, a number reached early in the marriage and maintained, although which two couples the marital pair were friendly with might have changed.

306. _____ and Ballweg, John A. "Black Family Structure and Primary Relations". Phylon 33 (1972):334-47.

307. _____. "Primary Extended Kin Relations of Negro Couples". The Sociological Quarterly 12 (Winter 1971):69-77.

308. Babchuk, Nicholas and Bates, Alan P. "The Primary Relations of Middle-Class Couples: A Study in Male Dominance." American Sociological Review 28 (June 1963):377-84.

    Based on interviews with married couples living in Lincoln, Nebraska it was discovered that husbands (not wives) were more likely to initiate and determine mutual friendships.

309. Babchuk, Nicholas and Booth, Alan. "Voluntary Association Membership: A Longitudinal Analysis." American Sociological Review 34 (February 1969):31-45.

310. Backman, Carl W. and Secord, Paul F. "The Effect of Perceived Liking on Interpersonal Attraction." Human Relations 12 (November 1959):379-84.

311. Bacon, Sir Francis. "Of Friendship (1625)," pp. 15-21. In Classic Essays in English. Second edition. Edited by Josephine Miles. Boston: Little, Brown, 1965.

    Bacon restates Artistotle's theme of a true "friend is another self," but, to Bacon, a man is more than a social creature for whoever prefers solitude to society "is either a wild beast or a god." In this brief essay, Bacon concentrates on the openness that characterizes true friendship -- someone "to whom you may impart griefs, joys, fears, hopes, suspicions, counsels, and whatsoever lieth upon the heart to oppress it, in a kind of civil shrift or confession."

312. Baker, Luther G. "The Personal and Social Adjustment of the Never-Married Woman." Journal of Marriage and the Family 30 (August 1968):473-79.

313. Balswick, Jack. "Explaining Inexpressive Males: A Reply to L'Abate." Family Relations 29 (April 1980):231-33.

314. _____. "The Inexpressive Male: Functional-Conflict and Role Theory as Contrasting Explanations." The Family Coordinator 28 (July 1979):331-36.

   Sociologist Balswick presents and contrasts a role theory of male inexpressiveness with a functional-conflict model. The author suggests that male expressiveness will change if males devote more time to "emotion-laden roles," such as childrearing.

315. _____. "Why Husbands Can't Say 'I Love You.'" Woman's Day, 1974.

316. Barrett, Carol J. "Intimacy in Widowhood." Psychology of Women Quarterly 5 (Spring 1981):473-87.

   Psychologist Barrett, who has led widows groups, considers all the intimate relationships available to a widow -- friends, relatives, professionals, nonprofessional associates, the deceased spouse, God, and the widow herself. A review of the literature on widows and friends (pages 474-76) stresses the limitations in those relationships "when we consider that loneliness is the most consistent problem widows endure." The author ends with some intriguing questions for further research.

317. Bates, Alan P. and Babchuk, Nicholas. "The Primary Group: A Reappraisal". The Sociological Quarterly 2 (July 1961):181-91.

318. Bashor, Philip S. "Plato and Aristotle on Friendship." Journal of Value Inquiry 2 (Winter 1968):269-80.

   Philosopher Bashor, based on Lysis, as well as Plato's other relevant dialogues, interprets Plato's stance on friendship: "In spite of the fact that the ultimate origin, meaning, and purpose of such friendship relations are normally concealed from our distinct apprehension, we have sufficient reason to accept them and to believe in them, if they are pursued without physical abuse, for ideal aims, and subject to the constant corrective of <u>logos</u>."

319. Becker, Howard S. "Notes on the Concept of Commitment." <u>American Journal of Sociology</u> 66 (1960):32-40.

"...Commitments come into being when a person, by making a side bet, links extraneous interests with a consistent line of activity. Side bets are often a consequence of the person's participation in social organizations. To understand commitments fully, an analysis of the system of value within which side bets are made is necessary." (Abstract)

320. Becker, Howard S. and Useem, Ruth. "Sociological Analysis of the Dyad". <u>American Sociological Review</u> 7 (1942):13-26.

321. Beidelman, Thomas O. "The Blood Convenant and the Concept of Blood in Ukagaru." <u>Africa</u> 33 (1963):321-42.

322. Bell, Julian. "The Samaritan Concept of Befriending." <u>The British Journal of Social Work</u> 5 (Winter 1975):413-22.

323. Bell, Robert R. "Friendships of Women and of Men." <u>Psychology of Women Quarterly</u> 5 (Spring 1981):402-17.

A study by the author of <u>The Worlds of Friendship</u> that examines the responses of four groups of respondents divided by gender and their Conventionality or Nonconventiality of values and attitudes. Bell concluded that female friendships are "more personal and emotionally based than those of men" and that "Nonconventional women and men may have more in common than do Conventional and Nonconventional women or men."

324. Belo, Jane. "A Study of a Balinese Family". <u>American Anthropologist</u> 38 (1936):12-31.

325. Bensman, Joseph and Lilienfeld, Robert. "Friendship and

Alienation." Psychology Today, October 1979, pp. 56-57, 59-60, 63, 66, 114.

Sociologists Bensman and Lilienfeld comment on the importance of friendship today: "...friendship can perhaps compensate us for the loss of intimacy from what is widely perceived as an erosion of family, community, and other traditional institutions."

326. Berger, Peter L. and Kellner, Hansfried. "Marriage and the Construction of Reality: An Exercise in the Microsociology of Knowledge." Diogenes 46 (1964):1-25.

Sociologists Berger and Kellner see marriage as a stimulus to constructing a new reality; no other social relationship has as strong an effect. This redefinition of the world by the conjugal pair occurs through conversation; even former friendships are juggled and redefined because of the marital relationship.

327. Berkman, L. F. and Syme, Leonard. "Social Networks, Host Resistance, and Mortality: A Nine-Year Follow-up Study of Alameda County Residents." American Journal of Epidemiology 109 (1979):186-204.

The researchers found a definite relationship between social and community ties and mortality. Using the 1965 Human Population Laboratory survey of a random sample of 6,928 adults in Alameda County, California, and a 9-year mortality follow-up, the authors conclude that people who lacked social and community ties were more likely to die within the follow-up period than those with more extensive contacts. In every age category, people who reported having few friends and relatives and/or who rarely saw them, had higher mortality rates than those persons who had many friends and/or relatives and saw them frequently.

328. Bernikow, Louise. "Alone: Yearning for Companionship in America." New York Times Magazine, August 15, 1982, pp. 24-30, 32.

329. _____. "What's Special About Women's Friendships?"

Ms., June 1980, pp. 39-40, 42.

"In friendship," writes Bernikow, "women do for each other what culture expects them to do for men..."

330. Bigelow, Brian J. "Children's Friendship Expectations." Child Development 48 (March 1977):246-53.

Bigelow found support for his three-stage hypothesis about friendship development (situational, contractual, internal-psychological) from an analysis of 480 essays written by subjects ranging from the ages of 6 to 14 on what they "expected in their best friends that was different from other acquaintances."

331. _____. "Developmental Changes in the Conceptual Friendship Expectations Associated with Children's Friendship Preferences." Human Relations 33 (1980):225-39.

332. _____ and La Gaipa, John J. "The Development of Friendship Values and Choice." In Friendship and Social Relations in Children, pp. 15-44. Edited by H. C. Foot, A. J. Chapman, and J. R. Smith. New York: John Wiley & Sons Ltd., 1980.

The researchers found that less value is placed on good moral character in a best friend by 17-year-olds than by 13-year-olds; intimacy is emphasized by late adolescents more than by early ones.

333. _____. "Children's Written Descriptions of Friendship: A Multidimensional Analysis." Developmental Psychology 11 (1975):857-58.

334. Blau, Peter. "A Theory of Social Integration." American Journal of Sociology 65 (May 1960):545-556.

"Social integration prevails in a group if bonds of attraction unite its members. Persons interested in becoming integrated members of a group are under pressure to impress the other members that they would make attractive associates, but the resulting competition for popularity

gives rise to defensive tactics that block social
integration. A member who can provide valued services to
the others forces them to give up their defensive tendencies
and manifest their attraction to him; the process in which
his services are exchanged for their respect and deference
gives rise to social differentiation. Alternatively, one
who demonstrates his approachability obviates the need for
the defensiveness of others and thus frees them to express
their feelings of attraction to him; the process in which
his disclaimer of superordinate status is exchanged for
their acceptance gives rise to social integration.
Empirical data support the hypothesis that acceptance as a
peer depends on approachability as well as attractiveness."
(Abstract)

335. Blau, Zena. "Structural Constraints on Friendships in Old Age." American Sociological Review 26 (1961):429-39.

336. Block, Joel D. "Male Friendships: The Importance, The Obstacles," Bottom Line Personal, August 30, 1982, p. 14.

337. _____. "Successful Friendships: The Key Ingredients." Bottom Line Personal, February 14, 1982, pp. 16-7.

Psychologist Block, author of Friendship, says that the three ingredients of a healthy friendship are the freedom to be yourself, acceptance, and direct communication. Blaming others and excessive dependency are the ingredients most destructive to friendship.

338. Blum, Alan F. and McHugh, Peter. "The Social Ascription of Motives." American Sociological Review 36 (February 1971):98-109.

339. Bohannon, Paul. "The Six Stations of Divorce." In Divorce and After, pp. 33-62. Edited by Paul Bohannan. Garden City, NY: Anchor/Doubleday, 1970.

Anthropologist Bohannon sees divorce as a process of "six overlapping experiences" which includes: (1) the emotional divorce; (2) the legal divorce; (3) the economic divorce; (4) the coparental divorce; (5) the community divorce, surrounding the changes of friends and community

that every divorcee experiences; and (6) the psychic
divorce, with the problem of regaining individual autonomy.

340. _____. "Divorce Chains, Households of Remarriage, and
Multiple Divorcers." In Divorce and After, pp. 127-39.
Edited by Paul Bohannan. Garden City, NY: Anchor/Doubleday,
1970.

341. Booth, Alan. "Sex and Social Participation." American
Sociological Review 37(1972):183-92.

    Conclusions are based on an analysis of responses from
800 adults over the age of 45 residing in Lincoln and Omaha,
Nebraska. The degree and type of male and female
participation in voluntary associations, friendship dyads,
and kin relations were examined. Findings in regard to
friendship were that males had more friends than females,
but female friendships were "affectively richer."

342. Booth, Alan and Hess, Elaine. "Cross-Sex Friendship."
Journal of Marriage and the Family (February 1974):38-47.

    "The structural opportunities and normative constraints
affecting the cross-sex friendships of men and women were
explored. Interview data from 800 middle-aged and elderly
urban residents revealed that while only a minority report
cross-sex friends, they constitute a significant segment of
the interpersonal resources of a number of adults. Women
had fewer opportunities and were subject to more constraints
with respect to the formation of cross-sex friendship ties
than men." (Abstract)

343. Brennan, Tim. "Loneliness at Adolescence." In Loneliness:
A Sourcebook of Current Theory, Research and Therapy,
Chapter 17, pp. 267-90. Edited by Letitia Anne Peplau and
Daniel Perlman. New York: Wiley, 1981.

344. Brenner, Jeffrey and Mueller, Edward. "Shared Meaning in
Boy Toddlers' Peer Relations". Child Development 53
(1982):380-91.

    Two play groups, each with six boy toddlers, were

studied. Twelve identifiable themes were shared, most frequently "motor copy," "object exchange," and "objection possession struggle." Shared meaning was correlated with longer interactions.

345. Brody, Jane E. "Personal Health" (Loneliness). New York Times, April 6, 1983, p. C10.

A column highlighting the work on loneliness of such sociologists and psychologists as Weiss, Shaver, Russell, and Peplau. Brody notes the difference between loneliness and being alone and cites Russell's finding that, for young students, loneliness is tied to the absence of fulfilling friendships, but for the older student, it is tied to lacking a romantic relationship.

346. Brown, Carol A.; Feldberg, Roslyn; Fox, Elizabeth M.; and Kohen, Janet. "Divorce: Chance of a New Lifetime." Journal of Social Issues 32 (1976):119-33.

347. Brown, Irene Q. "Domesticity, Feminism, and Friendship: Female Aristocratic Culture and Marriage in England, 1660-1760." Journal of Family History 7 (Winter 1982):406-24.

Brown discusses the special place of friendship during the Enlightenment. "...Friendships involving mutual obligation were valuable at a time when high mortality and morbidity touched even the elite....Life was precarious. Friendships, including those between women, between husband and wife, brother and sister, and across generations, all became one way of guarding against the effects of the emotional vulnerability fostered by sudden deaths...."

348. Burns, Tom. "Friends, Enemies, and the Polite Fiction." American Sociological Review 18 (December 1953):654-62.

349. Byrne, Donn and Buehler, John A. "A Note on the Influence of Propinquity Upon Acquaintanceships." Journal of Abnormal Social Psychology 50 (1955):163-67.

350. Caldwell, Mayta A. and Peplau, Letitia Anne. "Sex Differences in Same-Sex Friendship." Sex Roles 8

(1982):721-32.

    In their study of college-age men and women, Caldwell and Peplau found qualitative sex differences in friendship patterns, although the number of friends and the frequency of contact were the same for both sexes. Based on questionnaire responses and self-reports, the researchers discovered that the girls emphasized "emotional sharing and talking" in their friendships; the boys stressed "activities and doing things together."

351. Candy, Sandra Gibbs; Troll, Lillain E.; and Levy, Sheldon G. "A Developmental Exploration of Friendship Functions in Women". <u>Psychology of Women Quarterly</u> 5 (Spring 1981):456-72.

    Based on an analysis of questionnaires of 172 women, the authors conclude that "...the three general factors which appear to order friendship functions of women between 14 and 80" are "intimacy-assistance," "power," and "status."

352. Cannon, Lynn Weber and Guy, Rebecca F. "Married Couples Sex Role and Perceived Friendship Relations". <u>Free Inquiry in Creative Sociology</u> 11 (May 1983):84-88.

    An reexamination of how husband and wife affect friendship selection and maintenance because of the contradictory findings of Babchuk and Bates (1963) and Bates (1965) versus Simon, Crotts, and Mahan (1970). Cannon and Guy studied 61 white married couples, divided by nontraditional versus traditional roles. In support of Simon, Crotts, and Mahan's findings, these researchers also found that wives were more active in the initiation of "couple" friendships. Sex role orientation, however, was an important factor in who maintained a friendship -- "...nontraditional females and traditional males perceive wives to be the most active in friendship maintenance while nontraditional males and traditional females perceive husband and wife as equally active in friendship maintenance."

353. Cash, Thomas F. "Does Beauty Make A Difference?" <u>CTFA</u>

Cosmetic Journal 12 (1980):25-28, 38.

Psychologist Cash discusses why it took social scientists so long to get around to studying physical beauty, and its effects, summarizing studies on the meaning of beauty, dating, mating, and attractiveness ratings, beauty and the self-fulfilling prophesy, and clinical applications and directions for research.

354. _____ and Burns, D. Steven. "The Occurrence of Reinforcing Activities in Relation to Locus of Control, Success-Failure Expectancies, and Physical Attractiveness." Journal of Personality Assessment 41 (1977):387-91.

355. _____ and Derlega, Valerian. "The Matching Hypothesis: Physical Attractiveness among Same-Sexed Friends." Personality and Social Psychology Bulletin 4 (April 1978):240-43.

356. _____; Gillen, Barry; and Burns, D. Steven. "Sexism and 'Beautyism' in Personnel Consultant Decision Making." Journal of Applied Psychology 62 (1977):301-10.

357. _____; Kehr, Jo Anne; Polyson, James; and Freeman, Valerie. "Role of Physical Attractiveness in Peer Attribution of Psychologial Disturbance." Journal of Consulting and Clinical Psychology 45 (1977):987-993.

358. Challman, Robert C. "Factors Influencing Friendship Among Preschool Children." Child Development 3: (1932):146-58.

359. Chambliss, William J. "The Selection of Friends." Social Forces (1965):370-80.

Based on an analysis of 140 subjects in a small group setting, Chambliss reports on the results of this test of his theory on friendship formation: "persons will prefer for friends those with whom they have experienced encounters which are validating, successful and effective." (VSE)

360. Clutton-Brock, Arthur. "On Friendship." In Selected Moden English Essays. London: Oxford University Press, 1925, pp. 257-60.

361. Coelho, George V. "A Guide to the Literature of Friendship: A Selectively Annotated Bibliography". Psychological Newsletter 10 (1959):365-94.

Coehlo mainly prepared this valuable annotated bibliography in conjunction with a Seminar on Interpersonal Relations in Cross-Cultural Perspective, directed by Professor Cora DuBois, in the Social Relations Department of Harvard University during 1954-55. The four broad categories that the bibliography covers include: humanistic, anthropological, psychological, and sociological. The author overviews references to friendship in classical literature as well as the Hebrew Scripture and the New Testament, anthropology and, country-by-country, contemporary cross-cultural comparisons, including China, India, Japan, Korea, Vietnam, Iran, Israel, Europe, North America, and Latin America. Five typescript pages are devoted to sociological writings on friendship, highlighting Lazarsfeld and Merton's paper as well as references to friendship by Sorokin, Festinger, Rossi, Simmel, Parsons, and Weber. The annotations for, and references to, friendship in psychological studies are more detailed and given twice as much space in this useful interdisciplinary literature review. In addition to a discussion of the materials in the unpublished Studies of Friendship, edited by Du Bois, Coelho cites, and reviews, the writings related to friendship of Freud, Maslow, Menninger, Sullivan, and lesser-known psychologists.

362. Cohen, Yehudi A. "Patterns of Friendship." In Social Structure and Personality, pp. 351-86. Edited by Yehudi A. Cohen. New York: Holt, Rinehart & Winston, 1961.

The author distinguishes four types of friendship: inalienable; close; casual; and expedient. Sixty-five societies (such as the Arapesh of Northwest New Guinea, Chagga of northeastern Tanganyika, Hopi of Arizona, Tallensi of the northern Gold Coast of Africa, Tikopia of Polynesia, Kwakiutl Indians of British Columbia, Lesu of New Ireland in Melanesia, and Cusun of North Borneo) were surveyed by Cohen. He notes at the conclusion of this chapter that his results contradict the anthropological approach to the study of friendship presented by S. N. Eisenstadt in "Ritualized

Personal Relations: Blood Brotherhood, Best Friends, Compadre, Etc.: Some Comparative Hypotheses and Suggestions."

363. Collins, Glenn. "Friendship: A Fact of Life for Toddlers, Too." New York Times, December 15, 1980, p. B16.

    Interviews with child friendship experts Drs. Zick Rubin and Robert L. Selman, among others.

364. Conner, Karen A.; Powers, Edward A., Ph.D; and Bultena, Gordon L. "Social Interaction and Life Satisfaction: An Empirical Assessment of Late-Life Patterns." Journal of Gerontology 34 (1979):116-121.

365. Cook, Karen S. and Emerson, Richard M. "Power, Equity and Commitment in Exchange Networks." American Sociological Review 43 (October 1978):721-39.

366. Cooper, John M. "Friendship and the Good in Aristotle." Philosophy Review 86 (July 1977):290-315.

367. Cowgill, Donald O. and Baulch, Norma. "The Use of Leisure Time by Older People." The Gerontologist 2 (1962):47-50.

368. Corsaro, William A. "'We're Friends, Right?': Children's Use of Access Rituals in Nursery School". Language in Society 8 (1979):315-36.

369. Cozby, P. C. "Self-disclosure: A Literature Review." Psychological Bulletin 79 (1973):73-91.

370. Darley, John M. and Berscheid, Ellen. "Increased Liking as a Result of the Anticipation of Personal Contact", Human Relations 20 (1967):29-40.

371. Dauer, Edward A. and Leff, Arthur Allen. "Correspondence: The Lawyer as Friend (Charles Fried's article)." Yale Law Journal 86 (1977):573-84.

372. Davidson, Lynne R. and Duberman, Lucile. "Friendship: Communication, and Interactional Patterns in Same-Sex Dyads". Sex Roles 8 (August 1982):809-22.

"Based on the classic work of Georg Simmel on dyadic intimacy and dependency and more recent work on self-disclosure, this study uses subjective accounts to compare same-sex dyadic friendships. Past research has neglected the important dimension of content. Thus, a major purpose was to specify three content levels of communication -- topical, relational, and personal -- and to determine sex differences in the range and primacy of these levels. In addition, seven interactional factors were identified: spontaneous communication, trust, nonverbal communication, dependency, shared value systems, conflict, and competition for power. The data reveal that women relate on all three levels, while men relate primarily on the topical level. Overall findings on the seven interactional factors reveal high congruence with traditional gender stereotypes. A serendipitous finding for both male and female dyads is that a particular individual is of less importance than a particular type of friendship. This suggests that friendship in modern society may be more tenuous than Simmel contended." (Abstract)

373. Davidson, Sherwin and Packard, Ted. "The Therapeutic Value of Friendship Between Women." Psychology of Women Quarterly 5 (Spring 1981):495-510.

To determine if best and "slight" same-sex friends were considered therapeutic, 42 students at the University of Utah and 29 of their best friends were studied (with a median length of 5 years for the friendship between the subjects and their best friends). The researchers conclude that both types of friends were perceived as therapeutic ("contributing to one's personal growth, support, or change"), with best friendships seen as more therapeutic than slight friendships.

374. Davis, E. Donald. "Helping Out When a Friend Loses a Job." Bottom Line Personal, May 15, 1981, pp. 7-8.

375. Derlega, Valerie and Chaikin, Alan. "Norms Effecting Self-disclosure in Men and Women." Journal of Consulting and Clinical Psychology 44 (1976):376-80.

376. Dickens, Wenda J. and Daniel Perlman. "Friendship Over the Life-cycle." In *Personal Relationships 2: Developing Personal Relationships*, Chapter 4, pp. 91-122. Edited by Steve Duck and Robin Gilmour. New York: Academic Press, 1981.

In this review chapter, the authors summarize the research on friendship during childhood, adolescence, adulthood, and old age. They synopsize two main approaches to friendship development: the Selman and Jacquette and the Bigelow and La Gaipa models. Dickens and Perlman also make this generalization: "...contact with friends declines during the adult stage of the life-cycle while contact with kin increases." This generalization in based on the assumption, however, that someone is married with a spouse and children present (which, with the increase in the delaying of first marriage and/or divorce is not always the case).

377. Douvan, Elizabeth and Adelson, Joseph. "Friendship." In *The Adolescent Experience*, chapter 6, pp. 174-228. New York: Wiley, 1966.

The authors echo Sullivan's (*The Interpersonal Theory of Psychiatry*) point that friendships during adolescence aid the maturing child who must begin to create a self outside the family: "The need is to define personal identity; to accomplish this, the youngster needs the assurance and mirroring offered by others of the same disposition," e.g., peers.
Gender differences in adolescent friendships were also found by the researchers. Boys sought someone who is "amiable and nice" and also "supporting in trouble"; girls sought someone who is "not a gossip" followed by "amiable and nice" and, least importantly, "supporting in trouble."

378. Duck, Steve. "The Personal Context: Intimate Relationships." In *The Social Psychology of Psychological Problems*. Edited by P. Feldman and J. Orford. Chichester: Wiley, 1980.

379. _____. "Personal Relationships Research in the 1980s: Towards an Understanding of Complex Human Sociality." *The*

Western Journal of Speech Communication 44 (Spring 1980):114-9.

380. _____. "Personality Similarity and Friendship Choices by Adolescents." European Journal of Social Psychology 5 (1975):351-65.

381. _____. "Personality Similarity and Friendship Choice: Similarity of What, When?" Journal of Personality 41 (1973):543-8.

382. _____. "Similarity and Perceived Similiarity of Personal Constructs as Influences on Friendship Choice." British Journal of Social and Clinical Psychology 12 (1973):1-6.

383. _____. "Toward a Research Map for the Study of Relationship Breakdown." In Personal Relationships 3: Personal Relations in Disorder, edited by R. Gilmour and S. Duck. New York: Academic Press, 1981.

384. _____. "A Typography of Relationship Disengagement and Dissolution." In Personal Relationships 4: Dissolving Personal Relationships, edited by S. Duck. New York: Academic Press, 1982.

385. Duck, Steve; Miell, D.; and Gaebler, Heather C. "Attraction and Communication in Children's Interactions" in Friendship and Social Relations in Children, edited by H. C. Foot, A. J. Chapman, and J. R. Smith. London: Wiley, 1980, pp. 107-112.

   In a review of the literature on children's friendships, the authors conclude that "peer interaction and friendship is based on, and in turn comes to serve the function of, self-validation."

386. Duck, Steve and Sants, Harriet. "On the Origin of the Specious: Are Personal Relationships Really Interpersonal States?" Journal of Social and Clinical Psychology (1983).

387. Dunphy, Dexter C. "The Social Structure of Urban Adolescent Peer Groups." Sociometry 26 (1963):230-46.

388. Eckerman, Carol O. and Whatley, Judith L. "Toys and Social Interaction Between Infant Peers." Child Development 48 (1977):1645-56.

"Claims that young infants fail to react in a social manner to one another and that toys preempt attention to peers were assessed by comparing the interactions observed between infant peers when they met in the presence of toys versus in their absence...The results document that infants as young as 10 months of age are responsive to the person and behavior of an unfamiliar peer and that they are no less responsive than older infants to the social versus nonsocial aspects of a novel setting." (Abstract)

389. Eder, Donna and Hallinan, Maureen T. "Sex Differences in Children's Friendships." American Sociological Review 43 (April 1978):237-50.

Based on longitudinal sociometric data from children in one fifth grade and four sixth grade classes, the authors conclude that the dyadic best friendships of the girls that they studied "remained consistently exclusive over the school year" whereas the dyadic best friendships of the boys "expanded to include newcomers."

390. Edney, Julian J. and Grundmann, Michael J. "Friendship, Group Size and Boundary Size: Small Group Spaces." Small Group Behavior 10 (February 1979):124-35.

391. Edwards, John N. "Familial Behavior as Social Exchange." Journal of Marriage and the Family (August 1969):518-26.

392. Edwards, John N. and Saunders, Janice M. "Coming Apart: A Model of the Marital Dissolution Decision." Journal of Marriage and the Family 43 (May 1981):379-89.

Sociologists Edwards and Saunders advance a theory of the marital dissolution decision, stated in the form of propositions, that might be considered in regard to friendship dissolution.

393. Ehrenreich, Barbara. "After the Breadwinner Vanishes

(The Male Revolt)". <u>The Nation</u>, February 26, 1983, pp. 225, 240-2.

    This excerpt from Ehrenreich's book, <u>The Hearts of Men: American Dreams and the Flight from Commitment</u> (Anchor Press/Doubleday, 1983) discusses how the collapse of the myth of the man as breadwinner is changing the work (economic) and romantic roles of women today. It is also changing their friendship patterns. Women are "to an extent..." looking "for emotional support and loyalty from other women, while remaining, in most cases, sexually inclined toward men."

394. Eichenbaum, Luise and Orbach, Susie. "Men -- Why They're So Dependent On You." <u>Cosmopolitan</u>, February 1983, pp. 177-8, 182-3, 226-7.

    See page 226 for a popularized discussion of male socialization and how (and why) male friendship patterns differ from female ones.

395. Eisenstadt, S.N. "Ritualized Personal Relations: Blood Brotherhood, Best Friends, Compadre, Etc.: Some Comparative Hypotheses and Suggestions." <u>Man</u> No. 96 (July 1956):90-96.

    Eisenstadt's anthropological thesis is that blood brotherhood, blood friendship, best friends, compadre relations, and the godparent relation in several peasant societies "...have some basic characteristics in common, although they vary in the intensity of these characteristics, and that these characteristics are related to some similar or parallel social conditions." The four common characteristics that these relations share are that they are "particularistic, personal, voluntary and fully institutionalized (usually in ritual terms)."

396. Emerson, Ralph Waldo. "Love" and "Friendship." In <u>Essays by Ralph Waldo Emerson</u>, pp. 121-56. New York: Harper & Row, 1951.

    Like Cicero's honesty, Emerson sees truth as one of the two basic element in a friendship; the other is tenderness.

Emerson did not think that friendship had to be of equal value, or intensity, for its participants. "It has seemed to me lately more possible than I knew," Emerson writes, "to carry a friendship greatly on one side, without due correspondence on the other...The essence of friendship is entireness, a total magnanimity and trust. It must not surmise or provide for infirmity. It treats its object as a god, that it may deify both." According to Emerson, sincerity is necessary for friendship, a quality hard to maintain between two people for, as Emerson notes, "Every man alone is sincere. At the entrance of a second person, hypocrisy begins."

397. Encyclopaedia of Religion and Ethics. Edited by J. Hastings. New York: Scribner's, 1914, 1969. "Friendship" by St. George Stock.

Includes a good survey of the Greco-Roman perspective on friendship.

398. Etzioni, Amitai. "Groups: The Sense of Belonging". New York Times, March 29, 1978, p. C1.

399. Fellin, Phillip and Litwak, Eugene. "Neighborhood Cohesion Under Conditions of Mobility." American Sociological Review 28 (1963):364-76.

400. _____. "The Neighborhood in Urban American Society." Social Work 13 (1968):72-80.

401. Festinger, Leon. "Architecture and Group Membership." Journal of Social Issues No. 7 (1951):152-63.

402. Fine, Gary Alan. "Friends, Impression Management, and Preadolescent Behavior" in The Development of Children's Friendships, edited by S. Asher and J. Gottman. Cambridge: Cambridge University Press, 1981.

Over a three-year period, Fine observed Little League baseball leagues in four American communities. Fine concluded: "Friendship is a crucial factor in the development of the social self, both for popular boys and for boys with few close friends."

403. _____. "The Natural History of Preadolescent Male Friendship Groups." In _Friendship and Social Relations in Children_, pp. 293-320. Edited by H.C. Foot, A. J. Chapman, and J. R. Smith. London: Wiley, 1980.

    For the preadolescent, Fine states emphatically: "Friendships characterize this period and may take priority over relations of kith and kin." The five cultural elements of friendship that Fine pinpoints and that relate to preadolescent friendships include: known; usable; functional; appropriate to the group's status system; and triggered by a specific event.

404. _____. "Small Groups and Culture Creation: The Idioculture of Little League Baseball Teams." _American Sociological Review_ 44 (October 1979):733-745.

405. Firth, Raymond. "Bond Friendship in Tikopia" in _Custom Is King: Essays Presented to R. R. Marett_, edited by L. H. Dudley Buxton, pp. 259-69. London: Hutchinson, 1936.

406. Fischer, Claude S. "The Public and Private Worlds of City Life." _American Sociological Review_ 46 (June 1981):306-16.

407. _____. "What Do We Mean By 'Friend': An Inductive Study". _Social Network_ 3(1982):287-306.

408. Fischer, Judith L. and Narus, Leonard J., Jr. "Sex Roles and Intimacy in Same Sex and Other Sex Relationships." _Psychology of Women Quarterly_ 5 (Spring 1981):444-55.

409. Foot, Hugh C.; Chapman, Anthony J.; and Smith, Jean R. "Introduction", pp. 1-11 in _Friendship and Social Relations in Children_, edited by H. C. Foot, A. J. Chapman, and J. R. Smith. New York: Wiley, 1980.

410. Fried, Charles. "The Lawyer as Friend: The Moral Foundations of the Lawyer-Client Relation." _Yale Law Journal_ 85 (1976):1060-89.

411. _____. "Author's Reply," Correspondence. _Yale Law_

Journal 86 (1977):584-87.

412. Fromm-Reichmann, Frieda. "Loneliness." Psychiatry 22 (February 1959):1-15.

   After discussing the difference between aloneness and loneliness, as well as the type of creative loneliness necessary for artistic or scientific work, psychiatrist Fromm-Reichmann discusses the inability of the lonely person to even talk about it, the stigma of loneliness, and emotional versus physical loneliness.

413. Furman, Wyndol. "Enhancing Popularity and Peer Relations in Children." In Personal Relationships 5: Repairing Personal Relationships. Edited by Steve Duck. London: Academic Press, 1984.

414. _____. "Promoting Appropriate Social Behavior: A Developmental Perspective." In Advances in Clinical Child Psychology, Volume 3. Edited by Benjamin Lahey and Alan Kazdin. New York: Plenum Press, 1981.

415. Furman, Wyndol; Rahe, Donald F., and Hartup, Willard W. "Rehabilitation of Socially Withdrawn Preschool Children through Mixed-age and Same-age Socialization." Child Development 50 (1979):915-22.

416. Gerson, Ann C. and Perlman, Daniel. "Loneliness and Expressive Communication". Journal of Abnormal Psychology 88 (1979):258-61.

417. Giele, Janet Zollinger. "Centuries of Womanhood: An Evolutionary Perspective on the Feminine Role." Women's Studies 1 (1972):97-110.

   Sociologist Giele highlights the key sex role formulations that "have prevailed at successive stages of societal evolution" including primitive and archaic sex roles, sex roles in early modern society, and modern or contemporary sex roles. Giele concludes: "...the consciousness of inequality with men that contemporary women feel was virtually impossible before the early modern era because until then, women did not share a broad enough base of experience with men to be able to compare their situations in universal terms." Her findings about the evolution of sex roles are relevant to a study of friendship since it could be predicted that the traditional sex role-related friendship patterns of women will be affected by their new roles. (This point is, indeed, advanced by S. Gordon in "The New Corporate Feminism.")

418. Goffman, Erving. "Embarrassment." American Journal of Sociology 62 (1956):264-71.

419. Goode, William J. "The Theoretical Importance of Love." American Sociological Review 24 (1959):38-47.

420. _____. "A Theory of Role Strain." American Sociological Review 25 (1960):483-96.

Goode's seminal article on role strain introduces a valuable concept in understanding why friendship, a seemingly optional role, might be resented for competing with such "necessary" roles as worker, spouse, or sibling.

421. Gottman, John M.; Gonso, Jenni; and Rasmussen, Brian. "Social Interaction, Social Competence and Friendship in Children." Child Development 46 (1975):709-18.

422. Gouldner, Alvin W. "The Norm of Reciprocity: A Preliminary Statement." American Sociological Review 25 (April 1960):161-78.

Gouldner's hypothesis that "a norm of reciprocity is universal" is an important consideration in the meaning of exchange in human behavior, in general, and in friendship, in particular.

423. Gordon, Suzanne. "The New Corporate Feminism". The Nation, February 5, 1983, pp. 1, 143, 146-7.

Journalist Gordon asserts that women are being told that to succeed in the corporate world "...they must overcome their feminine socialization" and, if necessary, exclude friends in the workplace. She quotes one guide as stating "'The separation of personal, private self from public self may be distasteful but most managers find it necessary.'" An article on office politics put it this way: "...you were hired to get the job done, not to win friends..." so that, concludes Gordon, "...friendships are inappropriate and sticking together must give way to looking out for number one, say the corporate Machiavellis."

424. Gove, Walter R. "Sex, Marital Status, and Mortality." American Journal of Sociology 79 (July 1973):45-67.

425. Granovetter, Mark S. "The Strength of Weak Ties." American Journal of Sociology 78 (May 1973):1360-80.

426. Graziano, William G. and Musser, Lynn Mather. "Initiation and Conduct of Relationships, and Parting of the Ways." In Personal Relationships 4: Dissolving Personal Relationships. New York: Academic Press, 1982.

427. Green, Elise Hart. "Friendships and Quarrels Among Preschool Children." Child Development 3 (1933):237-52.

Green studied nursery school friends and quarreling behavior of 21 boys and 19 girls, ranging in ages from 2 to 5 years. She observed that the number of friends increases from ages 2 to 3, and the depth of friendship increases from ages 3 to 5. Girls had slightly more friends, but boys formed deeper friendships. Boy-boy groups were most quarrelsome, boy-girl groups less quarrelsome, and girl-girl groups least quarrelsome. Whereas mutual friends were more quarrelsome, mutual quarrelers were more friendly than average.

428. Hacker, Helen Mayer. "Blabbermouths and Clams: Sex Differences in Self-Disclosure in Same-Sex and Cross-Sex Friendship Dyads". Psychology of Women Quarterly 5 (Spring 1981):385-401.

429. Hallinan, Maureen T. "Classroom Racial Composition and Children's Friendships". Social Forces 61 (September 1982):56-72.

430. Hartup, Willard W. "Children and Their Friends." In Issues in Childhood Social Development, chapter 5, pp.

130-70. Edited by H. McGurk. London: Methuen, 1978.

Child psychologist Hartup states the function of childhood friendships in strong terms: "Long-term longitudinal investigations demonstrate that peer relations in childhood are prognostic indicators of social conduct in adolescence and adulthood."

431. _____. "Peer Relations and the Growth of Social Competence." In The Primary Prevention of Psychopathology, vol. 3, pp. 150-70. Edited by M.W. Kent and J.E. Rolf. Hanover: University Press of New England, 1979.

"Social competencies derive from the child's intereactions with other children as well as from family interaction," Hartup states. The importance of friendship deserves as much attention as parent-child relations which used to dominate child psychology. "Good adjustment to the peer culture is facilitated by good family adjustment, but the contributions to socialization made through peer interaction are unique."

432. Hays, Robert B. "The Development and Maintenance of Friendship." Journal of Social and Personal Relationships 1 (March 1984):75-98.

433. Hess, Beth B. "Friendship and Gender Roles Over the Life Course," pp. 104-15. In Single Life. Edited by Peter J. Stein. New York: St. Martin's Press, 1981.

Hess summarizes the literature on gender differences in friendship patterns and also offers her opinion as to why this is so: girls are encouraged to be "...specialists in human relations, to develop few but highly emotional relationships -- and thus prepare to become mothers and wives who will invest much in a very limited set of others. Boys are expected to have extensive networks of buddies; to share all kinds of team experiences, typically goal-directed; to be gregarious -- precisely the type who should do well in the American occupational structure...In this sense, childhood socialization and the resulting friendship patterns adopted by boys and girls are highly functional to the adult roles they will assume, and highly preservative of societies."

434. _____. "Friendship." In *Aging and Society: Volume 3 (A Sociology of Age Stratification*, pp. 357-93. Edited by Matilda White Riley, Marilyn Johnson, and Anne Foner. New York: Russell Sage Foundation, 1972.

A valuable early review article on sociological contributions on the subject of friendship and their application to the study of the elderly. "A central theme of this essay is that the number and type of friendships open to an individual at particular stages of his life course depend less upon explicit age criteria for the friendship role itself than upon the other roles that he plays. As his total cluster of roles changes over his lifetime, so do his friendship relations undergo change." (That theme is consistent with the friendship-related perspective of the sociological studies of the elderly conducted by Zena Blau and Irving Rosow.) Hess also discusses friendship formation, duration, and disruption as well as direct and indirect contributions of friendship to the socialization of children, adolescents, adults, and the elderly.

435. Hill, Charles T.; Rubin, Zick; Peplau, Letitia Anne. "Breakups Before Marriage: The End of 103 Affairs." *Journal of Social Issues* 32 (1976):147-68.

The researchers, through questionnaires and interviews, conducted a two-year study of dating relationships among college students at four colleges in the Boston area. Their sample consisted of 231 couples. After citing how breakups before marriage differ from breakups after marriage, the authors note what light pre-marital dissolution can shed on the dissolution of any close relationship.

436. Homans, George C. "Social Behavior as Exchange." *American Journal of Sociology* 63 (May 1958):597-606.

Homans states his theory of exchange most clearly in this article -- that "...interaction between persons is an exchange of goods, material and non-material." An important concept in regard to friendship, and why, perhaps old friends are taken for granted and new ones sought out, is also expressed in this article, namely Homans' idea about satiation or "The more he gets, the less valuable any further unit of that value is to him..."

437. Hoopes, Margaret H. "Friendship, Singleness, and Human Intimacy." Family Perspective 17 (Winter 1983):41-50.

438. Horn, Jack C. "Relationships: In Cities, Fast Friends Come Slowly." Psychology Today, April 1981, pages 32, 100.

Horn reports on environmental psychologist Karen Franck's study, reported in volume 36 of the Journal of Social Issues. The results of an experiment with students who moved to New York City or to an upstate rural area led to the conclusion that "urban friendships, while harder to make, 'may be more intimate, more highly valued, or more emotionally intense than relationships in nonurban settings precisely because they are juxtaposed with so many impersonal contacts.'"

439. Hughes, Michael and Walter R. Gove. "Living Alone, Social Integration, and Mental Health." American Journal of Sociology 87 (July 1981):48-74.

440. Huston, Ted L. and Burgess, Robert L. "Social Exchange in Developing Relationships: An Overview," pp. 3-28. In Social Exchange in Developing Relationships. Edited by T.L. Huston and R.L. Burgess. New York: Academic Press, 1979.

441. Huston, Ted L. and Cate, Rodney M. "Social Exchange in Intimate Relationships," pp. 263-69. In Love and Attraction. Edited by M. Cook and G. Wilson. New York: Pergamon Press, 1979.

442. Huston, Ted L. and Levinger, George. "Interpersonal Attraction and Relationships," pp. 115-56 in Annual Review of Psychology, vol. 29. Edited by M.R. Rosenzweig & L.W. Porter. Palo Alto: Annual Reviews, 1978.

443. Huston, Ted L. and Robins, Elliot. "Conceptual and Methodological Issues in Studying Close Relationships".

Journal of Marriage and the Family 44 (November 1982):901-925.

444. Institute for Social Research, The University of Michigan. "Marriage vs. Single Life". ISR Newsletter, August 1982, p. 8.

445. _____. "Women's Well-Being at Midlife". ISR Newsletter, Winter 1982, pp. 5-6.

446. International Encyclopedia of the Social Sciences, 1968 edition. "Friendship" by Odd Ramsoy.

447. Irish, Donald P. "Sibling Interaction: A Neglected Aspect in Family Life Research". Social Forces 42 (March 1964):279-88.

448. Izard, Carroll E. "Personality Similarity and Friendship." In Approaches, Contexts, and Problems of social Psychology. Edited by Edward E. Sampson. Englewood Cliffs, N.J.: Prentice-Hall, 1964, pp. 113-8.

449. Jacklin, Carol Nagy and Maccoby, Eleanor E. "Social Behavior at Thirty-three Months in Same-Sex and Mixed-Sex Dyads." Child Development 49 (1978):557-69.

   The authors found that 33-month-olds were more free in their play when paired with those of the same sex.

450. Jackson, Jacquelyne Johnson. "Comparative Life Styles and Family and Friend Relationships Among Older Black Women." Family Coordinator (1972):477-85.

451. Jackson, Robert Max. "Social Structure and Process in Friendship Choice," pp. 59-79. In Networks and Places: Social Relations in an Urban Setting. Edited by Claude S. Fischer, et al. New York: Free Press, 1977.

   This chapter discusses "the extent to which the structural positions of the Detroit respondents <in their friendship study> influences their choice of friends and, in particular, their selection of friends in social positions similar to their own." How friends are similar in a variety of contexts -- neighborhood, voluntary associations, childhood, work -- are discussed as well as the possible reasons for the similarities or dissimilarities. Jackson concludes: "Social similarity in friendship is significant not only in its intrinsic relevance for understanding social networks but also for understanding the general stratification of society. Segregation in social networks is the manifestation in informal social structure of a society's formal structure."

452. Jacobson, David. "Fair Weather Friend: Label and Context in Middle-Class Friendships." Journal of Anthropological Research 31 (1975):225-34.

453. Jacoby, Susan. "Friends: Those You Can Count on...Those You Can't." Cosmopolitan, November 1983, beginning p. 260.

454. _____. "Hers." New York Times, July 24, 1980, p. C2.

In this column on friendship, journalist Jacoby makes a plea that as women give up their care-giver role, which, according to the author, "is the cornerstone of women's friendship," that they not lose their friendship advantage (over men). According to the author, this is, unfortunately, beginning to occur. "The number of women who are workaholics -- especially among those without children -- is growing...I know a number of women who, having discovered the joys of work at a later period of life than I did, are now giving love and friendship short shrift in their pursuit of professional success."

455. Jecker, Jon and Landy, David. "Liking a Person as a Function of Doing Him a Favor." Human Relations 22 (1969):371-78.

456. Johnson, Michael P. "Social and Cognitive Features of the Dissolution of Commitment to Relationships." In Personal Relationships 4: Dissolving Personal Relationships. New York: Academic Press, 1982.

457. Johnson, Michael P. and Leslie, Leigh. "Couple Involvement and Network Structure: A Test of the Dyadic Withdrawal Hypothesis." Social Psychology Quarterly 45 (1982):34-43.

These sociologists studied the network involvements of 419 university students who were engaged in romantic relationships ranging from occasional dating through marriage. In support of the dyadic withdrawal hypothesis, the authors found that as a couple became more involved romantically, "their friendship networks shrink and they become less involved with those friends who remain in the network." By contrast, kin networks do not diminish, yet, as might be predicted, "the variance in number of kin listed increases dramatically at engagement and again at marriage."

458. de Jong-Gierveld, Jenny and Aalberts, Monique. "Singlehood: A Creative or a Lonely Experience?" Alternative Lifestyles 3 (August 1980):350-68.

459. Jones, Stella B. "Geographic Mobility as Seen by the Wife and Mother". Journal of Marriage and the Family (May 1973):210-18. Reprinted in The Research Experience, edited by M. Patricia Golden. Itasca: Peacock Publishers, 1976, pp. 315-27.

460. Jourard, Sidney. "Healthy Personality and Self-disclosure." Mental Hygiene 43 (1959):449-507.

461. Kadushin, Charles. "The Friends and Supporters of Psychotherapy: On Social Circles in Urban Life." American Sociological Review 31 (1968):786-802.

462. _____. "Networking: No Panacea". J. C. Penny Forum (March 1983), pp. 18-19.

463. _____. "Notes on Expectations of Reward in N-Person Networks." In Continuities in Structural Inquiry, pp. 235-54. Edited by Peter M. Blau and Robert K. Merton. Beverly Hills: Sage, 1981.

464. Kaufman, Debra Renee. "Associational Ties in Academe: Some Male and Female Differences." Sex Roles 4 (1978):9-21.

Interviews were conducted with 46 females and 32 males who had the rank of assistant professor or higher in a college of human ecology in a large northeastern university. Respondents were asked to list all faculty members whom they considered to be colleague-friends. An analysis of the data revealed that female professors, especially those who were unmarried, had fewer males in their collegial-friend networks than did the male professors. "Whether by choice or exclusion, it is suggested that isolation from these informal collegial contacts leaves women at a professional disadvantage."

465. Klemesrud, Judy. "'Girlfriends' Director on Female Friendship." New York Times, August 4, 1978, p. A12.

   Interview with Claudia Weill, director of the film, "Girlfriends." The film was about what happened when one of two roommates moves out to get married. "What I tried to do was show that female friendship is as fragile, delicate, supportive, complex, nourishing, painful and difficult as a love affair," explained Weill.

466. Knupfer, Genevieve, M.D.; Walter Clark, M.A.; and Robin Room, M.A., "The Mental Health of the Unmarried." American Journal of Psychiatry (February 1966):841-51.

467. Kobrin, Frances E. and Hendershot, Gerry E. "Do Family Ties Reduce Mortality? Evidence from the United States, 1966-1968." Journal of Marriage and the Family 39 (November 1977):737-45.

468. Kon, Igor S. and Losenkov, Vladimir A. "Friendship in Adolescence: Values and Behavior." Translated by Charlotte De Lissovoy and Vladimir De Lissovoy. Journal of Marriage and the Family (February 1978):143-55.

469. Krain, Mark. "Effects of Love and Liking in Premarital Dyads." Sociological Focus 10 (August 1977):249-262.

470. L'Abate, Luciano. "Inexpressive Males or Overexpressive Females? A Reply to Balswick." Family Relations 29 (April 1980):229-30.

471. La Gaipa, John J. "Children's Friendships." In Developing Personal Relationships, pp. 159-83. Edited by Steven Duck and Robin Gilmour. New York: Academic Press, 1981.

La Gaipa notes that Bigelow's research gave some support "...for the notion that the FD (friendship expectations) dimensions would fall into three distinct sets representing developmental stages: reward-costs; normative; and empathy."

472. _____. "A Developmental Study of the Meaning of Friendship in Adolescence." Journal of Adolescence 2 (1979):201-13.

473. _____. "A Systems Approach to Personal Relationships," pp. 67-89 in Personal Relationships. Edited by Steve Duck and Robin Gilmour. London: Academic Press, 1981.

474. _____. "Testing a Multidimensional Approach to Friendship," pp. 249-70. In Theory and Practice in Interpersonal Attraction. Edited by Steve Duck. London: Academic Press, 1977.

475. Larson, Reed W. "Adolescents' Daily Experience with Family and Friends: Contrasting Opportunity Systems." Journal of Marriage and the Family (November 1983):739-50.

Based on a stratified random sample of 75 high school students providing self-reports at random times. "The findings suggest that friendship interactions are experienced as positive feedback systems, having a high potential for fluid interchange but also lower homeostasis and a propensity to get out of control." (Abstract)

476. Lazarsfeld, Paul F. and Merton, Robert K. "Friendship as Social Process: A Substantive and Methodological Analysis." In Freedom and Control in Modern Society, pp. 18-66. Edited by Morroe Berger, Theodore Abel, and Charles H. Page. New York: D. Van Nostrand, 1954.

In their well-known essay on friendship homophily, sociologists Lazarsfeld and Merton took "like attracts like" a step further. They emphasized that although it is true that like attracts like ("status homophily"), the concept is far more complex and could also include "value homophily." Their insights are based on a secondary analysis of their studies of two housing projects (one in New Jersey and one in Pennsylvania), studies that they carried out for a larger study, <u>Patterns of Social Life: Exploration in the Sociology and Social Psychology of Housing</u>, a study that was, in fact, never published.

Based upon their respondents' answers to questions about their values, such as racial values, the authors generalized their findings to establish this concept: those with similar values will become friends. Those with dissimilar values will not become friends, or if they do become friends, one person will deemphasize the contrasting value or avoid a confrontation on that issue. The authors put it this way: "...for the friends, by virtue of their attachment, are strongly motivated to modify their values in the service of easing strains on the relationship. In the cumulative give-and-take of the friendship, initial divergences of value tend to be reduced."

477. Lever, Janet. "Sex Difference in the Complexity of Children's Play and Games." <u>American Sociological Review</u> 43 (August 1978):471-83.

Sociologist Lever, based on a one-year study of 181 fifth grade children, concluded that "Boys' play is more complex than girls' play, as indexed by such attributes as role differentiation, interdependence between players, size of play group, explicitness of goals, number of rules, and team formation."

478. _____. "Sex Differences in the Games Children Play." <u>Social Problems</u> 23 (1976):478-87.

479. Levi-Strauss, Claude. "The Principle of Reciprocity." In <u>Sociological Theory</u>, 4th ed., pp. 61-70. Edited by Lewis A. Coser and Bernard Rosenberg. New York: Macmillan, 1976.

480. Levinger, George. "A Social Psychological Perspective on Marital Dissolution." <u>Journal of Social Issues</u> 32 (1976):21-47.

In words that echo the exchange perspective, Levinger discusses the attractions of a dyad (that which holds a couple together), the barriers to divorce that keep a dyad intact, versus the alternative attractions (friends, co-workers, family) that may weaken the marital relationship and provoke its termination. Levinger concludes: "...people stay in relationships because they are attracted to them and/or they are barred from leaving them, and that, consciously or not, people compare their current relationships with alternative ones. If internal attraction and barrier forces become distinctly weakened than those from a viable alternative, the consequence is breakup..." Although friendship is not an exact functional equivalent to marriage, there are parallels in the attractions of one friendship, versus dissolving it or forming another, that might be considered in light of Levinger's analysis.

481. _____. "Task and Social Behavior in Marriage." Sociometry 27 (1964):433-48.

482. Lewin, Kurt. "Some Social-psychological Differences between the U.S. and Germany" in Kurt Lewin, Resolving Social Conflicts. New York: Harper & Row, 1948.

In his essay on "Friendship," Zick Rubin (see Unpublished section for reference) points out that, as reflected in Lewin, "the impression persists that Americans tend to have superficial 'friendships' with many people, while Europeans tend to have deeper 'friendships' with fewer people."

483. Lewis, Robert A. "Emotional Intimacy Among Men." Journal of Social Issues 34 (1978):108-21.

Lewis, who has conducted intimacy workshops at men's conferences since 1975, discusses why males lack same-sex friendships that are "close, intimate, or characterized by self-disclosure" even if males have a greater number of same-sex friends.

484. Libby, Roger W. "Creative Singlehood as a Sexual Life-Style: Beyond Marriage as a Rite of Passage." In Marriage and Alternatives, pp. 37-61. Edited by R.W. Libby and Robert N. Whitehurst. Glenview, IL: Scott, Foresman, 1977.

485. Litwak, Eugene. "Occupational Mobility and Extended Family Cohesion." American Sociological Review 25 (1960a):9-21.

486. Litwak, Eugene and Szelenyi, Ivan. "Primary Group Structures and Their Functions: Kin, Neighbors, and Friends." American Sociological Review 34 (August 1969):465-81.

> Data from Hungary and the United States are used to support the authors' hypothesis that "because of differences in structure, neighbors can best handle immediate emergencies; kin, long term commitments; and friends, heterogeneity."

487. Lopata, Helena Znaniecka. "Friendship: Historical and Theoretical Introduction," pp. 1-19. In Research in the Interweave of Social Roles: Friendship, A Research Annual. Vol. 2. Edited by Helena Z. Lopata and David Maines. Greenwich, CT: JAI Press, 1981.

488. _____. "Loneliness: Forms and Components." Social Problems 17 (1969):248-61.

489. Lowenthal, Marjorie Fisk. "Social Isolation and Mental Illness in Old Age." American Sociological Review 29 (1964):54-70.

490. Lowenthal, Marjorie Fisk and Haven, Clayton. "Interaction and Adaptation: Intimacy as a Critical Variable." American Sociological Review 33 (1968):20-30.

> The authors studied 280 residents of San Francisco, aged sixty and over, and concluded that "...if you have a confidant, you can decrease your social interaction and run no greater risk of becoming depressed than if you had increased it. Further, if you have no confidant, you may increase your social activities and yet be far more likely to be depressed than the individual who has a confidant but has lowered his interaction level." A confidant was defined as "a stable intimate relationship"; confidants were equally distributed among friends, spouses, and children.

491. Maas, Henry S. "Preadolescent Peer Relations and Adult Intimacy." Psychiatry 31 (1968):161-72.

492. Martin, Dawson. "The Lawyer as Friend." Rutgers Law Review 32 (1980):695-718.

493. Masello, Robert. "Can You Really Be Friends With an Ex-Lover?" Mademoiselle, September 1980, pages 90+.

494. Mayer, John E. "The Self-Restraint of Friends: A Mechanism in Family Transition." Social Forces 35 (1957):230-38.

495. Mead, Margaret. "Different Lands, Different Friendships." Redbook, August 1966, page 38+.

496. McAdams, Dan P. and Losoff, Michael. "Friendship Motivation in Fourth and Sixth Graders: A Thematic Analysis." Journal of Social and Personal Relationships 1 (March 1984):11-27.

497. McCallister, Lynne and Fischer, Claude S. "A Procedure for Surveying Personal Networks". Sociological Methods & Research 7 (November 1978):131-49.

498. McCall, George and Simmons, Jerry. "The Career of a Relationship." In Identities and Interactions, chapter 7, pp. 167-201. Edited by G. McCall and J. Simmons. New York: Free Press, 1966.

499. McPherson, Miller and Smith-Lovin, L. "Women and Weak Ties: Differences by Sex in the Size of Voluntary Organizations." American Journal of Sociology (January 1982).

500. Mercer, Marilyn. "Office Friendships: How They Really Affect Your Career". Glamour, April 1979, pp. 152, 154, 157.

A cautionary view of female friendships at the office as potentially troublesome for career advancement. "If you're looking for a promotion, belonging to a clique is not advisable," Mercer writes. A career counselor is quoted as warning, "Forming a close, mutual support, let-your-hair-down relationship with another woman in your office is a potentially explosive situation."

501. Miell, Dorothy; Duck, Steve; and La Gaipa, John. "Interactive Effects of Sex and Timing in Self-disclosure." British Journal of Social and Clinical Psychology 18 (1979):355-62.

502. Milgram, Stanley. "The Small World Problem." Psychology Today, 22 (1967):61-7.

503. Miller, Arthur A., M.D. "Reactions of Friends to Divorce." In Divorce and After, pp. 63-86. Edited by Paul Bohannan. Garden City, NY: Anchor/Doubleday, 1970.

   Miller remarks on friendship groups and discusses the feelings and thoughts of friends of divorcees as well as a consideration of the actions of divorcees' friends, based on their feelings, thoughts, and fantasies. Questions are raised, such as when and why do friends, overtly or subconsciously, act to subvert, or preserve, a marriage?

504. Montaigne. "Of Friendship." In The Complete Essays of Montaigne, pp. 135-44. Edited and translated by Donald M. Frame. Stanford: Stanford University Press, 1958.

   Building upon the themes of Aristotle and Cicero, Montaigne proposes that, first and foremost, man needs friendship. Friendship must be between equals; in an unequal relationship, respect may exist, but not friendship. Similarly, the affection for women cannot be categorized as friendship. Like Aristotle, Montaigne found women incapable of friendship. Montaigne does not believe that one can have more than one close friend for "If two called for help at the same time, which one would you run to?" Like Cicero, Montaigne sees having a genuine friend like having a "second self."

505. Mueller, Edward. "Fostering Peer Relations in Young Normal and Handicapped Children." In The Social Life of Children in a Changing Society. Edited by Kathryn M. Borman. Hillsdale, N.J.: Lawrence Erlbaum Associates, 1982.

506. _____. "The Maintenance of Verbal Exchanges Between Young Children." Child Development 43 (1972):930-8.

507. Murstein, Bernard I.; Cerreto, Mary; and MacDonald, Marcia G. "A Theory and Investigation of the Effect of Exchange-Orientation on Marriage and Friendship." Journal of Marriage and the Family (August 1977):543-48.

   The psychologists constructed an "exchange-orientation scale" (as well as marriage adjustment and friendship intensity scales) and administered the scales to married couples and same-sex friendship pairs at Connecticut College. The authors concluded that the most content marriages were those between two nonexchange-oriented persons (NE); the least satisfactory marriages were between two high exchange-oriented persons (E). They also found two high exchange-oriented persons (E) most content in their situationally determined friendships in the college dormitory. The authors seemed to have pursued an exchange theory orientation in their conclusion that in a long-term romantic relationship, the lower the expectations for the exchange, the higher the contentment with the relationship. By contrast, in a short-term friendship relationship situationally determined by proximity and necessity -- attending college together and becoming roommates -- an orientation toward high expectations and exchanges creates the momentum for initiating and perpetuating the relationship.

508. Murstein, Bernard I. and Spitz, Leah T. "Aristotle and Friendship: A Factor-Analytic Study." Interpersonal Development 4 (1973/74):21-34.

509. Naegele, Kaspar D. "Friendship and Acquaintances: An Exploration of Some Social Distinctions." Harvard Educational Review 28 (1958):232-52.

   In addition to expressing comparable view to Suttles' on the similarities and differences between marriage and friendship, Naegele notes that friendship "implies some kind of reciprocated closeness between two or more people who are free not to be close."

510. Nelson, Joel I., "Clique Contacts and Family Orientations." *American Sociological Review* 31 (October 1966):663-72.

511. Nemy, Enid. "Lunch for Women: Food and Ideas". *New York Times*, April 6, 1983, p. C8.

   Journalist Nemy reports on the trend toward women-only friendship lunches and dinners.

512. Neugarten, Bernice L. "Time, Age, and the Life Cycle." *American Journal of Psychiatry* 136 (July 1979):887-894.

513. Newcomb, Theodore M. "The Prediction of Interpersonal Attraction." *The American Psychologist* 11 (November 1956):575-86.

   In this classic work on friendship formation, Newcomb reports on controlled experiments that he conducted to substantiate the age-old notion about relationships, namely that "birds of a feather flock together" and the more recent proposition of propinquity, or "other things equal, people are most likely to be attracted toward those in closest contact with them." To test out his predictions, Newcomb interviewed two groups of 17 male transfer students at the University of Michigan, who had spent a semester together, with assigned roommates, in a rent-free student house. Newcomb concluded: "...one can predict to interpersonal attraction, under specified conditions, from frequency of interaction, from the perception of reciprocated attraction, from certain combinations of personality characteristics, and from attitudinal agreement."

514. Oden, Sherri and Asher, Steven R. "Coaching Children in Social Skills For Friendship Making." *Child Development* 48 (June 1977):495-506.

   Can children be taught how to develop, or to improve, their friendship skills? The experiments conducted by Oden and Asher indicate that when third and fourth grade socially isolated children were coached in social skills, such as cooperation, communication, participation, and validation support -- being fun, nice, and friendly -- they made

notable strides in peer acceptance, gains that were
maintained when retested a year later.

515. Oskamp, Stuart and Perlman, Daniel. "Effects of
Friendship and Disliking on Cooperation in a Mixed-motive
Game". Journal of Conflict Resolution 10 (1966):220-26.

516. Packard, Vance. "Have You Made Any New Friends Lately?"
Readers' Digest, February 1960, pages 55-8.

517. Paine, Robert. "In Search of Friendship: An Exploratory
Analysis in 'Middle-Class' Culture." Man new series 4
(December 1969):505-24.

   The two objectives of social anthropologist Paine's
article are to distill what is meant by the word friendship
when his colleagues use it (is "cousin behavior" kin or
friend behavior?) and "the tradition of structural analysis
in our discipline is surely indispensable when trying to
compare the nature and function of friendship with those of
other interpersonal relations to which it is close in one
way or another." Paine concludes that "...the making and
breaking of friendships in our society is largely a matter
of personal choice that is beyond social control."
Relationships in middle-class cultures that are less than
friendship are also discussed, such as acquaintanceship,
partnerships, professional relationships, patron-client
relations, group fellowship, and relations among kin and
between spouses.

518. Parlee, Mary Brown and Psychology Today editors. "The
Friendship Bond: PT's Survey Report." Psychology Today,
October 1979, pp. 43-54, 113.

   A report on the results of the March 1979 survey of
40,000 respondents to Psychology Today's friendship poll.
Although the problems with the unrepresentative nature of
the sample must be kept in mind, there is a wealth of
information on friendship, drawn on a sample size not
previously available. One of the findings, for example,
points out just how important an effect marriage has on
pre-existing friendships. In listing the thirteen most
common reasons that a friendship ended, the fourth and fifth
most frequent reasons related to marriage: "One of us got

married" and "My friend became involved with (or married) someone I didn't like."

519. Parsons, Talcott. "The Kinship System of the Contemporary United States." <u>American Anthropologist</u> 45 (January-March 1943):22-38.

520. Pearlin, Leonard I. and Johnson, Joyce S. "Marital Status, Life-Strains and Depression." <u>American Sociological Review</u> 42 (October 1977):704-15.

521. Pearlin, Leonard I. and Schooler, Carmi. "The Structure of Coping." <u>Journal of Health and Social Behavior</u> 19 (March 1978):2-21.

522. Perlman, Daniel; Gerson, Ann C.; and Spinner, Barry. "Loneliness Among Senior Citizens: An Empirical Report." <u>Essence</u> 2 (1978):239-48.

Studying loneliness among 158 senior citizens living in Winnipeg, Manitoba, Canada, the authors found less friendship contact and fewer close friends among the six factors associated with greater loneliness. (The other factors included: social anxiety, ineffectiveness in influencing others, low marital satisfaction, and low life satisfaction.)

523. Perlman, Daniel, and Peplau, Letitia Anne. "Toward a Social Psychology of Loneliness", chap. 2, pp. 31-56. In <u>Personal Relationships 3: Personal Relationships in Disorder.</u> Edited by R. Gilmour and S. Duck. New York: Academic Press, 1981.

An excellent review of the research on loneliness including a definition of the concept, how others react to lonely people, and ways to alleviate loneliness.

524. Petrowsky, Marc. "Marital Status, Sex, and Social Networks of the Elderly." <u>Journal of Marriage and the Family</u> 38 (November 1976):749-56.

525. Phillips, Derek L. "Social Participation and Happiness."

American Journal of Sociology 72 (March 1967):479-88.

526. Pines, Maya. "New Focus on Narcissism Offers Analysts Insight Into Grandiosity and Emptiness." New York Times, March 16, 1982, pp. C1,3.

527. Pitt-Rivers, Julian. "Ritual Kinship in Spain." Transactions, 2nd series 20 (1958):424-31. (New York Academy of Sciences)

528. _____. "Pseudo-kinship." International Encyclopedia of the Social Sciences. Volume 8, pp. 408-13. Edited by David L. Sills. New York: Macmillan & Free Press, 1968.

   The author distinguishes three types of pseudo-kin relationships (whereby persons are described by kin terms but are not kin by either descent or marriage): 1) the figurative use of kin terms; 2) when one is given the status of kinship by attribution or birth; and 3) ritualized forms of friendship. These three categories blend together and the structure of ritual kinship is characterized, not by birth "...but from the mutual feelings of individuals, guaranteed by the magical power of blood or the sacrosanctity of the rite."

529. Plath, David W. "Contours of Consociation: Lessons from a Japanese Narrative." In Life-Span Development and Behavior: Vol. 3, pp. 287-305. New York: Academic Press, 1981.

530. Pleck, Joseph H. "Man to Man: Is Brotherhood Possible?" pp. 229-44. In Old Family/New Family. Edited by Nona Glazer-Malbin. New York: D. Van Nostrand, 1975.

   Pleck looks at male sociability, versus intimacy, and how male-male relationships change during childhood, adolescence, and adulthood.

531. Pool, Ithiel de Sola, and Kochen, Manfred. "Contacts and Influence". Social Network 1 (1978):5-51.

   Written about twenty years previously and circulated in manuscript form, the authors admit to raising more questions than they answer in trying to assess someone's "acquaintance volume" or "the chance that they will have a friend in common."

532. Population Reference Bureau. "The Domestic Life of Americans." <u>Inter-Change</u> 6 (May 1977), p. 1.

533. Potashin, Reva. "A Sociometric Study of Children's Friendships." <u>Sociometry</u> 9 (1946):48-70.

534. Powers, Edward A. and Bultena, Gordon L. "Sex Differences in Intimate Friendships of Old Age." <u>Journal of Marriage and the Family</u> (November 1976):739-747.

   The authors concluded that men had more frequent social involvements than women, but a smaller number of those contacts were with intimate friends.

535. Redl, F.; Gump, P.; and Sutton-Smith, Brian. "The Dimensions of Games," pp. 408-18. In <u>The Study of Games</u>. Edited by Elliott M. Avedon and Brian Sutton-Smith. New York: Wiley, 1971.

536. Reina, Ruben E. "Two Patterns of Friendship in a Guatemalan Community," pp. 215-22. In <u>Society and Self</u>. Edited by Bartlett H. Stoodley. Glencoe, IL: Free Press, 1962.

537. Reisman, John M. and Yamokoski, T. "Psychotherapy as Friendship: An Analysis of the Communication of Friends." <u>Journal of Counseling Psychology</u> 21 (1974):269-73.

538. Renshaw, Peter D. and Asher, Steven R. "Social Competence and Peer Status: The Distinction Between Goals and Strategies", Chapter 16, pp. 375-95 in K. H. Rubin and H. S. Ross, eds., <u>Peer Relationships and Social Skills in Childhood</u>. New York: Springer-Verlag, 1982.

539. Richardon, H. M. "Community of Values as a Factor in Friendships of College and Adult Women." <u>Journal of Social Psychology</u> 11 (May 1940):303-12.

540. Roberts, John M. "Kinsmen and Friends in Zuni Culture: A

Terminological Note." <u>Palacio</u> 72 (1965):38-43.

541. Rodin, M. J. "Liking and Disliking: Sketch of an Alternative View." <u>Personality and Social Psychology Bulletin</u> 4 (July 1978):473-8.

542. Rollin, Betty. "Hers." <u>New York Times</u>, August 12, 1982, p. C2.

    TV/print journalist Rollin writes about how her relationships at work became her family, even more than friends, like "sisters."

543. Rollins, Judy. "A Conceptual and Theoretical Differentiation Between Loneliness and Aloneness." <u>Family Perspectives</u> 17 (Winter 1983):29-34.

544. Rose, Arnold M. <u>Sociology: The Study of Human Relations</u>. New York: Knopf, 1956. "The Friendship Group", pp. 174-9.

545. Rosen, Bernard C. and Aneshensel, Carol S. "The Chameleon Syndrome: A Social Psychological Dimension of the Female Sex Role", <u>Journal of Marriage and the Family</u> 38 (November 1976):605-17.

546. Rosenblatt, Roger. "Friends and Countrymen." <u>Time</u>, July 21, 1980, pp. 50, 53.

547. Rosow, Irving. "Old People: Their Friends and Neighbors." <u>American Behavioral Scientist</u> 14 (1970):59-69.

548. Rubin, Zick. "Breaking the Age Barrier to Friendship." <u>Psychology Today</u>, 1980, pp. 96+.

549. _____. "Seeking a Cure for Loneliness." <u>Psychology Today</u>, October 1979, pp. 82, 85-86, 89-90.

550. Rubin, Zick and Peplau, Letitia Anne. "Who Believes in a Just World?" <u>Journal of Social Issues</u> 31 (1975):65-90.

551. Rubin, Zick and Shenker, Stephen. "Friendship, Proximity, and Self-disclosure." <u>Journal of Personality</u> 46 (1978):1-22.

552. Ryan, John. "Marital Status, Happiness, and Anomia."

Journal of Marriage and the Family 43 (August 1981):643-49.

553. Safilios-Rothschild, Constantina. "Toward a Social Psychology of Relationships." Psychology of Women Quarterly 5 (Spring 1981):377-84.

"The paper examines the structural and socio-psychological factors which have led to the emergence of new types of relationships such as cross-sex colleagueships and cross-sex friendships and to a new value placed on intimacy. Because people are now involved in a wide range of relationships, studies of relationships should start from the individuals, map all the relationships in which they are involved and examine the interrelations between the different types of relationships...." (Abstract)

554. Salamon, Sonya. "Family Bounds and Friendship Bonds: Japan and West Germany." Journal of Marriage and the Family 39 (November 1977):807-20.

555. Schonberg, William B. and Potter, Hannah C. "Friendship Fluctuation in Senescence." Journal of Genetic Psychology 129 (December 1976):333-4.

556. Schwartz, Barry. "The Social Psychology of the Gift." American Journal of Sociology 73 (July 1967):1-11.

557. Seiden, Anne M. "Sex Roles, Sexuality, and the Adolescent Peer Group." In Annals of the American Society for Adolescent Psychiatry. New York: Basic Books, 1976.

558. Seiden, Anne M. and Bart, Pauline B. "Woman to Woman: Is Sisterhood Powerful?" In Old Family/ New Family, pp. 189-228. Edited by M. Glazer. New York: Van Nostrand Reinhold, 1975.

The authors present stereotypical views of female friendships as well as a discussion of women's friendships and family structure and a review of female friendships over the life cycle. There is a summary of findings from the interviews with twelve feminists about female friendship that the authors conducted, and the special issues about friendship that the women's movement raised.

559. Selman, Robert L. and Selman, Anne P. "Children's Ideas About Friendship: A New Theory." *Psychology Today*, October 1979, pp.71-72, 74, 79-80, 114.

A popular discussion of the five stages in childhood friendship in the Selman model, namely: "Momentary Physical Playmate," ages three to seven: "One-Way Assistance," ages four to nine; "Fairweather Cooperation," ages six to twelve; "Intimate-Mutual Sharing," ages nine to fifteen; and "Autonomous Interdependence," from age twelve on.

560. Sharabany, R. "Girlfriend, Boyfriend: Age and Sex Differences in Intimate Friendship." *Developmental Psychology* 17 (1981):800-08.

561. Shulman, Norman. "Life-Cycle Variations in Patterns of Close Relationships." *Journal of Marriage and the Family* 37 (November 1975):813-21.

In analyzing interviews with 347 adults between the ages of 18 and 65, including singles, Shulman found that singles, when ranking kin, friends, and neighbors for importance in their personal networks, were least likely to name any kin.

562. Simmel, Georg. "Friendship, Love and Secrecy". Translated by Albion Small. *American Journal of Sociology* 11 (1906):457-66.

563. _____. "The Metropolis and Mental Life." pp. 19-30 in *Urban Place and Process: Readings in the Anthropology of Cities*. Edited by Irwin Press and M. Estellie Smith. New York: Macmillan, 1980. (Reprinted from *The Sociology of Georg Simmel*, edited by K. Wolff, pp. 409-24.)

German sociologist Simmel's classic statement, written around 1903, on the impersonal nature of cities, compared to rural life. His insights about city life, unlike those that he made about the nature of the dyad and the triad, are somewhat dated as more recent studies have revealed that, in some cities, one block may interact in ways mirroring a rural community. (Nor does Simmel address the quasi-city, the suburbs.)

564. Simon, Rita James; Crotts, Gail; and Mahan, Linda. "An Empirical Note About Married Women and Their Friends." Social Forces 48 (June 1970):520-25.

  Based on interviews with only the wives of middle- and working-class couples, the authors discovered that the middle-class women had more friends as a couple than did working-class women. (Working-class wives spent more time alone with their friends, without their husbands present.) The male-dominance theme, reported by Babchuk and Bates, was not found by these researchers, although they qualify that finding by noting it might have emerged if they had also interviewed husbands.

565. Smith-Rosenberg, Carroll. "The Female World of Love and Ritual: Relations between Women in Nineteenth-Century America." Signs: Journal of Women in Culture and Society 1 (Autumn 1975):1-29.

  Basing conclusions on an analysis of correspondence and diaries of women and men in 35 families in the United States between the 1760s and 1860s and noting the importance of friendship, Smith-Rosenberg writes: "sisters, cousins and friends frequently accompanied newlyweds on their wedding nights and wedding trip, which often involved additional family visiting."

566. Sojourner: The New England Women's Journal of News, Opinions, and the Arts. "What Are Friends For?" October 1983. (Cambridge, MA)

  Most of this issue of this tabloid is devoted to friendship and includes the following articles: "What Is 'Romantic Friendship'?" by Susan Shapiro; "We've Been Friends Since We Were Four" by Sarah Swartz; "Drawing My Friendship Network" by Anita Fast; "Can Women and Men Really Be Friends?" by Leslie G. Baeren; "Nurturing Both Babies and Friends" by Leila Joseph; "Female Friendships on TV" by Karen Lindsey. Most of the articles are first-person essays by non-experts.

567. Somers, Anne R. "Marital Status, Health, and Use of Health Services: An Old Relationship Revisited." Journal of the American Medical Association 241 (April 27, 1979):1818-22.

568. Spock, Benjamin. "How Children Learn to Make Friends." Redbook, November 1972.

569. Starr, Joyce R. and Carns, Donald E. "Singles in the City." Society, February 1972, pp. 43-48.

570. Stein, Harry. "Just Good Friends." Esquire, August 1980, pp.21-23.

571. _____. "Looking Hard At Number One." Esquire, February 1981, pp. 20-21.

572. Stein, Peter J. "The Lifestyles and Life Chances of the Never-Married: A Review of the Recent Literature." Marriage & Family Review 1 (July/August 1978):1, 3-10.

573. Stone, Gregory P. "The Play of Little Children," pp. 4-17 in Child's Play. Edited by R. E. Herron and Brian Sutton-Smith. New York: Wiley, 1971.

574. Stueve, C. Ann and Gerson, Kathleen. "Personal Relations Across the Life-Cycle" in Networks and Places, edited by Claude Fischer. New York: Free Press, 1977.

   The authors reexamined The Detroit Area Study of 1965-66 in the light of friendship over the life cycle. Reinterpreting the data on close friendships, as reported by the 985 white males between the ages of 21 and 64 in the original sample, they concluded: "Marriage and parenting seemed to pull men away from childhood friendships and toward friendships formed in adulthood...Close ties formed in the neighborhood and at work became the major substitutes for the childhood friends left behind...young husbands had fewer local friends than did young single men. But upon the birth of the first child, the neighborhood again became an important source of friends."

575. Sutcliffe, J.P. and Crabbe, B.D. "Incidence and Degrees of Friendship in Urban and Rural Areas." Social Forces 42 (October 1963):60-67.

576. Tesich, Steve. "Focusing on Friends." New York Times Magazine, December 4, 1983, p. 162.

> In this first-person essay, screenwriter ("Breaking Away") Tesich echoes the gender differences in friendship that social scientists like Lewis have described: "Therein lies the difference, I think, between my friendships with men and with women. I can tell women I love them. Not only can I tell them, I am compulsive about it. I can hardly wait to tell them. But I can't tell the men. I just can't. And they can't tell me. Emotions are never nailed down...."

577. Tesser, Abraham and Smith, Jonathan. "Some Effects of Task Relevance and Friendship on Helping: You Don't Always Help the One You Like." Journal of Experimental Social Psychology 16 (1980):582-90.

578. Thompson, Linda and Walker, Alexis J. "The Dyad as the Unit of Analysis: Conceptual and Methodological Issues". Journal of Marriage and the Family 44 (November 1982):889-900.

579. Tognoli, Jerome. "Male Friendship and Intimacy Across the Life Span." Family Relations 29 (July 1980):273-79.

580. Tomeh, Aida K. "Birth Order and Friendship Associations". Journal of Marriage and the Family (August 1970):360-69.

581. Toomey, D.M. "Conjugal Roles and Social Networks in an Urban Working Class Sample." Human Relations 24: (1971):417-31.

582. Tuma, N. B. and Hallinan, Maureen. "The Effects of Sex, Race, and Achievement on Schoolchildren's Friendships." Social Forces 57 (June 1979):1265-83.

583. Turner, R. Jay. "Social Support as a Contingency in Psychological Well-Being." Journal of Health & Social Behavior 22 (December 1981):357-67.

584. Udry, Richard and Hall, Mary. "Marital Role Segregation and Social Networks in Middle-Class Middle-Aged Couples." Journal of Marriage and the Family 27 (August 1965):392-95.

585. Vaughan, Diane. "Uncoupling: The Social Construction of Divorce." In Social Interaction, pp. 323-38. Edited by Robboy, Greenblatt, and Clark. New York: St. Martin's Press, 1979.

In a continuation of Berger and Kellner's description of how marriage redefines reality for the couple, Vaughan traces the stages a couple goes through when the process is reversed in preparation for divorce. Although the author means her analysis to apply to any heterosexual relationship, not just marriage, it is intriguing to ponder what, if any, application there is to the termination of an intimate same-sex friendship dyad.

586. Verbrugge, Lois M. "Marital Status and Health." Journal of Marriage and the Family 41 (May 1979):267-85.

587. _____. "Multiplexity in Adult Friendships." Social Forces 57 (June 1979):1286-1309.

Multiplexity is defined as "the overlap of roles, exchanges, or affiliations in a social relationship." Verbugge, whose dissertation was on friendship contact, looks at how adult friendship dyads in a Detroit and West German city overlap in three affiliations: kin, neighbor, and co-worker.

588. _____. "The Structure of Adult Friendship Choices." Social Forces 56 (December 1977):576-97.

Verbrugge used two cross-sectional sample surveys of adult populations in Detroit and a West German city. Respondents in both studies (1,013 males and 820 males and females, respectively) were asked to name his or her three best non-kin friends. The author concludes: "Compared to a random-choice model, adult friendships show strong bias toward status similarity for all social characteristics...The less similar two people are in social characteristics, the less likely they are to be close friends."

589. Weinberg, S. Kirson. "Primary Group Theory and Closest Friendship of the Same Sex: An Empirical Analysis", chapter 22, pp. 301-19 in Human Nature and Collective Behavior, ed. Tamotsu Shibutani. Englewood Cliffs, NJ: Prentice-Hall, 1970.

590. Weiss, Robert S. "The Emotional Impact of Marital Separation." Journal of Social Issues 32 (1976):135-45.

591. Weissman, Myrna M. and Paykel, Eugene S. "Moving and Depression in Women." Society 9 (July/August 1972):24-8.

   This study of women in New Haven, Connecticut, who were being treated at a clinic for depression, discusses how even voluntary relocations cause depression with the separation from old friends as an important factor in their current emotional states.

592. Williams, James H. "Close Friendship Relations of Housewvies Residing in an Urban Community". Social Forces 36 (May 1958):358-62.

   Based on interviews with 411 high and low status married women residing in Columbia, South Carolina, the author concluded: (1) high status women had more close friends than lower status women; (2) those housewives who belonged to a greater number of organizations or clubs had more close friends; (3) younger and older wives had more close friends than those in the intermediate age group; and (4) lower status women met more of their close friends in their neighborhood than did high status wives.

593. Williams, Robin M. "Friendship and Social Values in a Suburban Community: An Exploratory Study." The Pacific Sociological Review 2 (1959):3-10.

594. Winslow, C. N. "A Study of the Extent of Agreement Between Friends' Opinions and Their Ability to Estimate the Opinions of Each Other." Journal of Social Psychology 8

(November 1937):433-42.

595. Wirth, Louis. "Urbanism as a Way of Life". <u>American Journal of Sociology</u> 44 (1938):1-24.

596. Wolf, Eric R. "Kinship, Friendship, and Patron-Client Relations in Complex Societies" in <u>The Social Anthropology of Complex Societies</u>. Edited by M. Banton. London: Tavistock, 1966.

597. Wolfe, Linda. "Friendship in the City." <u>New York</u>, July 18, 1983, pp. 20-8.

598. "Women Are Their Own Worst Friends" in <u>Science Digest</u>, August 1976, pp. 8-9.

599. Wong, Herbert. "Typologies of Intimacy." <u>Psychology of Women Quarterly</u> 5 (Spring 1981):435-43.

    A discussion of some of the elements that would have to be taken into account to create typologies or ideal types for a definition of intimacy in romantic and friendship relationships, including the concepts of self-disclosure, communication and negotiation, exclusiveness, and duration.

600. Wood, Vivian and Robertson, Joan F. "Friendship and Kinship Interaction: Differential Effect on the Morale of the Elderly". <u>Journal of Marriage and the Family</u> (May 1978):367-75.

    The authors interview 257 working-class grandparents living in Madison, Wisconsin. Their findings, consistent with that of Arling, Lowenthal, Powers, Bultena, and others, were that friends were more important than grandchildren "for maintaining morale in old age."

601. Wright, Paul H. "The Development and Selected Applications of a Conceptual and Measurement Model of Friendship." In <u>Families and Close Relationships: Individuals in Social Interaction</u>. Edited by J. L. Fischer. Lubbock, TX: Texas Tech University Press, 1983.

602. _____. "Toward a Theory of Friendship Based on a

Conception of Self." Human Communication Research 4 (1978):196-207.

603. _____. "Self-referent Motivation and the Intrinsic Quality of Friendship." Journal of Social and Personal Relationships 1 (March 1984):115-30.

UNPUBLISHED MATERIALS: CONFERENCES, CORRESPONDENCE, PAPERS, REPORTS, AND AUDIO-VISUALS

Unpublished papers may be available from the authors (or they may advise you that it has been published in a journal or book that you could easily locate). If you need to contact authors, directories of the pertinent professional organizations (listed in the next section, "Organizational Resources") may have the address that you need. For audio-visual materials, the name of the company or organization that produced the film, as well as the city in which it is located, is listed. If necessary, consult a phone directory or contact a telephone operator, if you need to contact the distributor directly.

As sociology attends to friendship and related themes (self-disclosure, loneliness, children's play), there will surely be more related audio-visual materials available to educators, researchers, and interested layman. At the present time, there is far more audio-visual material on the family and other traditional units in the sociology curriculum (stratification, social change, discrimination, etc.).

604. Adolescence: A Case Study. (20 minutes; color; film). New York: CRM/McGraw-Hill Films, 1978.

605. Are You Listening/Widows (28 minutes; color; film and videocassette) Hillsdale, N.Y.: Martha Stuart Communications.

   A group of widows share their experiences, expressing their grief and anger.

606. Asher, Steven R. and Wheeler, Valerie A. "Children's Loneliness: A Comparison of Rejected and Neglected Peer Status." Paper presented at the annual meeting of the American Psychological Association, Anaheim, California,

1983.

607. Babchuk, Nicholas, Regents Professor of Sociology, University of Nebraska-Lincoln. "Select Bibliography on Primary Relations (Intimacy, Confidants, Networks, Neighbors, Friends)". University of Nebraska, Didactic Seminar, January 1979.

608. Berndt, Thomas J. "Why Do Children's Friendships End: Problems with Levels of Analysis." Paper presented at the First International Conference on Personal Relationships, Madison, Wisconsin, July 1982.

609. Big Boys Can Cry. Produced by Francine Achbar; directed by Chuck O'Neill and Bill Huggins. (28 minutes; color; film and videocassette) Northbrook, IL: MTI Teleprograms, 1982.

    A discussion of the changes in American society because of the women's movement and how those evolving sex roles are affecting men.

610. Bigelow, B. J. "Disengagement and Development of Social Concepts: Toward a Theory of Friendship." Paper presented at the First International Conference on Personal Relationships, Madison, Wisconsin, July 1982.

611. Du Bois, Cora, ed. Studies of Friendship. Unpublished, Department of Social Relations, Harvard University, September 1955.

    Includes a review of the psychological literature on friendship, by Willa D. Abelson and Elizabeth J. Weiss, "Psychological Studies of Friendship." George V. Coelho devotes four pages of his "A Guide to Literature on Friendship" review in Psychological Newsletter (see entry 361) to a summary and abstracts from that paper reviewing 93 psychological studies on friendship.

612. Cash, Thomas F. "Self-disclosure in Initial Acquaintanceship: Effects of Sex, Approval Motivation, and Physical Attractiveness." Manuscript dated 1978; received 1982.

613. Duck, Steve and Miell, Dorothy. "Charting the Development of Personal Relationships." Paper presented at the First International Conference on Personal Relationships, Madison, Wisconsin, July 1982.

614. Duck, Steve and Perlman, Dan, eds. The Sage Series in Personal Relationships, Volume I. Beverly Hills,: Sage, 1984-5. (in press)

    See especially Keith Davis and Michael J. Todd, "Prototypes, Paradigm Cases, and Relationship Assessment: The Case of Friendship" and Dan P. McAdams, "A Motivational Approach to the Study of Friendship".

615. Eggleston, Lynn, Search Analyst, New York State Library Data Base Services. "Why Marriage Ends, Divorce, Causes of Divorce." Dissertation Abstracts 1861 - March 1981, 21 April 1981; Psychological Abstracts (PSYC), 1967 - February 1981, 17 April 1981; Social Science Citation Index (SSCI), 1965 - February 1981, 17 April 1981; Sociological Abstracts (SA), 1965 - February 1981, 17 April 1981.

616. Epstein, J. L. "Choice of Friends Over the Life Span: Developmental and Environmental Influences." Chapter to appear in Edward Mueller and Catherine Cooper, eds., Process and Outcomes in Peer Relations. New York: Academic Press, in press.

617. _____. "Reexamining Theories of Adolescent Friendships with Longitudinal Data." Paper read at Session 199 on Socialization at the annual meeting of the American Sociological Association, Boston, 1979.

618. Erwin, P. G. "Similarity of Attitudes and Constructs in Children's Friendships". Paper delivered at the First International Conference on Personal Relationships, University of Wisconsin at Madison, July 1982.

619. Etzkowitz, Henry and Stein, Peter J. "The Life Spiral: Social Change and Life Structures." Paper presented at the annual meeting of the Eastern Sociological Society, Philadelphia, April 1978.

620. Farrell, Michael. "Artists' Circles and the Development

of Artists." Paper presented at the annual meeting of the American Sociological Association, August 1980.

621. Farrell, Michael and Rosenberg, S. "Male Friendship and the Life Cycle." Paper presented at the annual meeting of the American Sociological Association, 1977.

622. Feshbach, Norma D. "Empathy Training: A Field Study of Affective Education." Paper presented at the annual meeting of the American Educational Research Association, Toronto, 1978.

623. Fischer, Claude S., Principal Investigator. Questionnaire for Northern California Communities Study. Survey Research Center, Institute of Urban and Regional Development. Berkeley: University of California, 1977.

624. Fischer, Claude S. and Oliker, Stacey J. "Friendship, Sex, and the Life Cycle." Unpublished working paper. Berkeley: Institute of Urban and Regional Development, University of California, March 1980.

Network analysts Fischer and Oliker examined the number of friendships of 1,050 adults in six life stages (young singles, married, parents with one or more children under 18 at home; middle-aged parents, middle-aged couples without children, and the elderly). They concluded that the number of friends differed for men and women depending upon the life cycle stage. For young marrieds and parents, men had more friends than women, but women had more friends at the empty-nest and elderly stages. The early differences are explained by structural factors (the sexual division of labor at home and the type of work that women tended to do give less incentive for work-related friendships) and the later differences by dispositional factors (once structural constraints on women are reduced, their inclination toward larger friendship networks can be realized).

625. Fitzpatrick, Mary Anne and Bochner, Arthur. "Insider and Outsider Perspectives on Self and Other: Male-Female Differences in the Perceptions of Interpersonal Behaviors." Manuscript of paper for publication in Sex Roles, vol. 7, 1981.

626. Fitzpatrick, Mary Anne and Indvik, Julie. "The Cause of Conceptual Clarity: An Explication and Elaboration of the Basic Dimensions of Relational Life." Paper presented at the annual meeting of the Speech Communication Association, New York, 1980.

627. Furman, Wyndol, Department of Psychology, University of Denver. "The Acquaintanceship Process in Middle Childhood." Ms. received April 1984.

628. <u>A Gang Ain't Nothin' But Friends</u>. (29 minutes; black-and-white) Philadelphia, PA: WCAV-TV.

629. Gurdin, J. Barry. "Friendship Between Nurses and Their Patients - A Typical Case Study." Paper and talk presented as part of the session on "Bridging the Gap from Hospital to Home" at the annual conference of the Association of Rehabilitation Nurses, Chicago, October 1979.

630. _____. "Themes from Amitie/Friendship: The Socio-cultural Construction of Friendship in Contemporary Montreal/Brief Report on Recent Research." Paper presented at the annual meeting of the American Anthropological Association, Cincinnati, Ohio, 1979.

631. Gurdin, J. Barry and Hutter, Horst. "Some of My Best Friends Are...The Relationship of Ethnicity to Close Friendship." Paper presented at the annual meeting of the Society for the Study of Social Problems (SSSP), Detroit, 1983.

   Deals with the results of a random sample of over 1,000 residents of Montreal, looking at their friendship patterns. A major finding was that there was a strong tendency for ethnic homophily among close friends for certain ethnic groups.

632. Hacker, Helen M. "The Influence of Gender Roles on Reciprocal Patterns in Same-Sex and Cross-Sex Friendship Dyads". Paper presented at the IXth World Congress of Sociology, I.S.A. Uppsala, Sweden, August 1978.

633. Hymer, Sharon. "Narcissistic Friendships". Unpublished paper, received May 1982.

After a brief discussion of the classical theories of friendship as reflected in the thoughts of Aristotle, Cicero, and Zeno, clinical psychologist Hymer explores the concept of narcissism and then, through detailed reporting on two case histories, shows how working through a narcissistic friendship can be useful in analysis. Hymer notes that "to date, both theoretical formulations and clinical studies have paid scant attention to the significant self-objects <u>outside</u> the narcissistic patient's family of origin," and that working with friendship relationships can be beneficial in treatment.

634. Indvik, Julie. "The Variable Nature of Relationships at Work: The Influence of Job Level, Career Stage, and Competence on Peer and Superior-Subordinate Relationships." Paper presented at the First International Conference on Personal Relationships, Madison, Wisconsin, July 1982.

635. <u>Interpersonal Influence</u>. (30 minutes; color) Lincoln, NB: Nebraska Educational TV Council for Higher Education, 1971.

636. Johnson, Michael P. "Personal and Structural Commitment: Sources of Consistency in the Development of Relationships." Paper presented at Pre-conference Theory and Methods Workshop, annual meetings of the National Council on Family Relations, Philadelphia, 1978.

Sociologist Johnson defines personal commitment to a relationship to consist of three components: satisfaction with the relationship itself; definition of self in terms of the relationship; an internalized sense of moral obligation to the maintenance of the relationship.

637. de Jong-Gierveld, Jenny. "Loneliness and the Degree of Intimacy in Personal Relationships." Paper presented at the First International Conference on Personal Relationships, Madison, Wisconsin, July 1982.

638. La Gaipa, John J. "Life Stages and the Termination of Friendship." Paper presented at the symposium, "The Development and Termination of Friendship," at the meeting

of the Southeastern Psychological Association, Washington, D.C., March 1980.

639. La Gaipa, John J. and Bigelow, Brian. "The Development of Childhood Friendship Expectations." Paper presented at the Canadian Psychological Association, 1972.

640. Landberg, Michelle. "Age, Self-concept and Sex as Predictors of Friendship Expectations in Adolescence." Paper presented at the First International Conference on Personal Relationships, Madison, Wisconsin, July 1982.

641. Kadushin, Charles. "Frontiers of Research in Network Theory and Method." Paper delivered at the AAAS Meetings in Houston, January 1979.

642. McCaffrey, Erika, Search Analyst, New York State Library Data Base Services. "Sociology of Friendship." Sociological Abstracts, 1963 - present, 29 October 1980; Dissertation Abstracts and Psychological Abstracts, 1935 - present, 30 October 1980; Social Sciences Citation Index, 1977 - present, 5 November 1980.

643. Mettetal, Gwendolyn, Communications Department, Purdue University. "Intimate Conversations: Self-Disclosure in the Natural Conversations of Friends." Paper presented at the First International Conference on Personal Relationships, Madison, Wisconsin, July 1982.

"In this study, females of three age groups (6 to 7 years old, 11 to 12 years old, and 16 to 17 years old) were videotaped as they engaged in free conversation with a best friend or an acquaintance....High intimacy disclosure was more likely in friends than acquaintances, thus supporting social penetration theory, but was seen primarily in the oldest group." (Abstract)

644. Miller, Gerald R. and Parks, Malcolm R. "Communication in Dissolving Relationships." (Typescript.) (Now published in Personal Relationships 4, edited by Steve Duck. See entry 81)

645. Noonan, John Ford. "A Coupla White Chicks Sitting Around Talking." Directed by Dorothy Lyman. Performance at Astor

Place Theatre, New York City, 5 August 1980.

A play about two neighbors in a suburb who spend time together in the city and the friendship that develops.

646. Oden, Sherri; Herzberger, Sharon; Mangione, Peter; and Wheeler, Valerie. "A Developmental Study of Children's Peer Relationship Formation". Paper presented at the International Conference on Personal Relationships, Madison, Wisconsin, July 1982.

Earlier portions of the research were presented at Boundary Areas in Psychology: Social and Developmental at Vanderbilt University, Nashville, Tennessee, June 1981.

647. Pearlman, Daniel and Peplau, Anne Letitia. "Loneliness Research: Implications for Interventions." Paper prepared for "Preventive Interventions to Reduce the Harmful Consequences of Loneliness" workshop sponsored by the Office of Prevention, National Institute for Mental Health (NIMH), 1982.

648. Potter, Ralph B. "Topics in the History of Ethics: Friendship." Unpublished paper, Harvard Divinity School, n.d.

This 19-page typescript is a wealth of references, annotations, and discussion of friendship from an ethical, historical, literary, philosophical, and social science viewpoint. The material is presented thematically and chronologically with summaries of the key perspective of the individual or discipline covered. Potter covers friendship in the Old and New Testaments as well as sixteenth century authors, "A Pessimist's View of Friendship" (Schopenhauer), and brief references to sociology, anthropology, ethnography, psychology, and political science. Written as a detailed course outline, Potter's citations and commentary are a significant contribution toward an overview of ethical, philosophical, and literary treatments of the theme through the ages.

649. _____. "Topics in the History of Ethics: Friendship."

Course outline, Harvard Divinity School, Spring, 1984.

A shortened four-page outline, with a supplementary reading list, synopsizing the material presented in Potter's more comprehensive version.

650. Risoli, Toni, Search Analyst, New York State Library Data Base Services. "Friendships Among Women." Sociological Abstracts, 1978 present, 22 April 1982.

651. _____. "Sociology of Friendship," Sociological Abstracts, 1963 - date, 22 April 1982.

652. Rubin, Zick. "Friendship" to be published in The Social Science Encyclopedia, edited by Adam and Jessica Kuper. (London: Routledge and Kegan Paul, in press.)

653. Second International Conference on Personal Relationships, July 1984, Madison, Wisconsin.

An interdisciplinary conference of psychologists, sociologists, and comunication analysts. Conference themes were: July 23 - Developmental Aspects of Relationships; July 24 - Communication in Relationships; July 25 - Relationships in Health and Illness; July 26 - Social and Structural Aspects of Relationships. Competitive papers, poster sessions, and symposium were presented and/or conducted.

654. Sixteen in Webster Groves. (47 minutes; black-and-white) New York: Carousel Films, 1966.

A film recommended by introductory sociology professors about the values of teenagers and how conformity is a prevailing concern. (There is also a film of the same community ten years later.)

655. Sklar, Kathryn Kish. "Female Relationships: Hypotheses for Future Research." Paper presented at the meetings of the American Studies Association, San Francisco, October 1973.

656. Smith-Rosenberg, Carroll. "The Woman's World of Love and Ritual." Paper presented at meetings of the Organization of American Historians, Denver, April 1974.

657. Social Animal. (30 minutes; black-and-white) New York: National Educational Television, 1963.

   Showing the experimental work of Festinger, Deutsch, and Schacter, this film's theme is how individuals are affected by group pressure.

658. Social Interaction. (30 minutes; color) Lincoln, NB: Nebraska Educational TV Council for Higher Education, 1969.

659. Stein, Peter J. "Men and Their Friendships," Paper presented at the Annual Groves Conference on Marriage and the Family, June 1982.

   Sociologist Stein discusses the results of an analysis of interviews with 40 middle-class professional white males. Friendship was important to this largely single group. "Despite the structural barriers and interpersonal limitations to male friendships mentioned above," Stein writes, "a number of men in our study found male friendships to be important and were committed to developing and sustaining friendships with other men."

660. _____. "Understanding Single Adulthood." Paper presented at the annual meeting of the National Council on Family Relations, Boston, August 1979.

661. Surra, Catherine, Department of Human Development and Family Ecology, University of Illinois, Urbana, Illinois. "From Courtship to Marriage: Patterns of Interaction between Partners and their Social Networks." Paper presented at the First International Conference on Personal Relationships, Madison, Wisconsin, July 1982.

662. Thurmond, Margaret, Guest Host. "Friendships." Guest: J. Barry Gurdin, Ph.D. 3/4" videotape. Los Angeles: Counseling Without Walls Foundation, 1982.

663. _____. "Friendships and Mental Health." Guest: J. Barry Gurdin, Ph.D. 3/4" videotape. Los Angeles:

Counseling Without Walls Foundation, 1982.

664. U. S. Department of Commerce, Bureau of the Census, Publication Information Office, Washington, D.C. "Changing Family Composition Associated With Lower Income Levels, Census Bureau Report Shows," "Commerce News", 22 September 1982 release.

665. _____. "Nation to Reach Zero Population Growth by 2050, Census Bureau Says in First Long-Range Projections Based on 1980 Census Results". "Commerce News", 9 November 1982 release.

666. _____. "Household Size Continues to Decline, Census Report Shows". "Commerce News", 19 November 1982 release.

667. Wheeler, Valerie A. "Reciprocity Within First Grade Friend and Nonfriend Dyads In a Conflict-of-Interest Situation." Paper presented at the First International Conference on Personal Relations, Madison, Wisconsin, July 1982.

668. Whitley, Bernard E.; Schofield, Janet Ward; and Snyder, Howard N. "Peer Preferences in a Desegregated School: A Round Robin Analysis." Paper accepted for publication pending minor revisions by Journal of Personality and School Psychology.

669. Wong, Paul T. P. and Derlega, Valerian. "An Attributional Analysis of Self-disclosure." Paper presented at the First International Conference on Personal Relationships, Madison, Wisconsin, July 1982.

670. Zaslow, Martha. "The Emergence of Peer Relations in Kibbutz Toddler Groups." Paper presented at the International Conference on Kibbutz Studies, New York City, June 1982.

ORGANIZATIONAL RESOURCES

The resources in this section provide a variety of services that readers of this friendship bibliography may find useful, including directories that may help in locating researchers or publications, newsletters about professional activities, upcoming friendship-related conferences, or self-help groups networking on issues related to friendship, resources for audio-visual materials, and information clearinghouses.

For help in finding local or state chapters or services, contact national organizations for referrals, or look in your local telephone directories for affiliate organizations in your area.

671. American Anthropological Association
    1703 New Hampshire Avenue, N.W.
    Washington, D.C. 20009

    Publishes <u>American Anthropologist</u>, a quarterly.

672. American Association of Marriage and Family Therapy
    924 West 9th Street
    Upland, California 91786

    Publishes a quarterly journal and bimonthly newsletter. Through its nationwide referral service provides assistance in finding a therapist.

673. American Psychiatric Association
    1700 18th Street, N.W.
    Washington, D.C. 20009

    Publishes a directory of members and numerous

journals.

674. American Psychological Association
1200 17th Street, N.W.
Washington, D.C. 20036

Publishes a bi-annual directory of members and several journals.

675. American Society for Adolescent Psychiatry
24 Green Valley Road
Wallingford, Pennsylvania 19086

676. American Sociological Association
1722 N Street, N.W.
Washington, D.C. 20036

For assistance in finding a sociologist. Publishes a directory of members, updated every two years, that may be purchased from the national office. Through its annual meeting, offers sociologists an opportunity to network and present research papers. Publishes a newsletter, <u>Footnotes</u>, for members, as well as numerous scholarly journals, such as <u>American Sociological Review</u> and <u>Journal of Health and Social Behavior</u>, where friendship-related research findings may be published.

677. American Studies Association
307 College Hall
University of Pennsylvania
Philadelphia, Pennsylvania 19104

Publishes <u>American Quarterly</u> and <u>American Studies International</u>.

678. Big Brothers/Big Sisters of America
117 South 17th Street
Suite 1200
Philadelphia, Pennsylvania 19103

Under the guidance of professional social workers,

adult volunteers are matched with children from single-parent homes. Volunteers are expected to see children about once a week, for four to six hours, for at least one year. The national headquarters will make referrals to local agencies and also answer inquiries about starting a new local agency.

679. Clinical Sociology Association
2 Wilburn Avenue
Atherton, California 94025

For help in finding a clinical sociologist. Publishes an annual directory of members as well as a monthly newsletter.

680. Compassionate Friends
P. O. Box 3247
Hialeah, Florida 33013

National coordinators for more than 100 chapters of this self-help peer network for parents whose children have died. At once a week rap sessions, parents aid each other in working through their grief.

681. CONTACT Teleministries USA, Inc.
900 South Arlington Avenue
Harrisburg, Pennsylvania 17109

A national organization with lay counselors throughout the country that staff telephone counseling services for information and referral, crisis intervention, and suicide prevention. The national headquarters will provide referrals to a local center; a national telephone directory includes all member centers.

682. Counseling Without Walls Foundation
1019 Gayley Avenue
Suite 102
Los Angeles, California 90024

A non-profit foundation with the motto "We Fight

America's #1 Cause of Premature Death -- Loneliness" with the goal of helping "people establish a personal resource supportive network of friends, activities and counseling in daily living" as well as "networking as an adjunct to therapy". "Friendship" and "Friendship and Mental Health," videotapes listed in the previous section on Unpublished Materials, may be rented or purchased from the foundation.

683. Family Service Association of America
44 East 23rd Street
New York, New York   10010

Founded in 1911, FSAA has about 300 member agencies located in 42 states. The national office makes referrals to local accredited agencies, which provide direct counseling services. Publishes journals for the professional counselor, such as Social Casework and The Family.

684. To Love and to Work: An Agency for Change
1450 East 55th Place
Suite 6285
Chicago, Illiois 60637

Director J. Barry Gurdin, Ph.D. facilitates friendship development groups.

685. National Association of Social Workers
1425 H Street, N.W. Suite 600
Washington, D. C. 20005

For help in finding a social worker. Updates its directory every few years.

686. National Self-Help Clearinghouse
33 West 42nd Street
Room 1227
New York, New York   10036

A clearinghouse of self-help groups throughout the country. Publishes a newsletter, Self-Help Reporter, and other materials; sponsors workshops and conferences on self-help.

687. Organization of American Historians
     112 N. Bryan Street
     Bloomington, Indiana 47401

     Publishes Journal of American History.

688. Parents Without Partners
     7910 Woodmont Avenue
     Suite 1000
     Washington, D.C. 20014

     Provides information about local chapters in the United States and Canada offering direct services to single-parent families. Publishes The Single Parent.

689. The Salvation Army
     National Headquarters
     50 West 23rd Street
     New York, New York 10010

     Through its local centers, residences, camps, telephone reassurance program, and social services, the Salvation Army provides opportunities for relationships. Free booklet available, "Where there was loneliness...Friendship."

690. SSRD Research Programme on Friendship Development
     Department of Psychology
     University of Lancaster
     Fylde College
     Bailrigg, Lancaster LA1 4YF England

     Director, Steve Duck, Ph.D. who is also editor of the Journal of Social and Personal Relationships, coordinates the bi-annual International Conference on Personal Relationships. The First and Second Conferences were held at the University of Wisconsin - Madison in July 1982 and 1984; the Third Conference is planned for Europe in 1986.

In addition to invited speakers, researchers and scholars present papers in the area of personal relationships, including friendship, from a variety of disciplines (sociology, social psychology, psychology, communication); offers an opportunity for networking with fellow researchers.

691. Stepfamily Association of America, Inc.
28 Allegeny Avenue
Suite 1307
Baltimore, Maryland 21204

    A national clearinghouse on stepfamilies, with local chapters throughout the United States, offering direct self-help and networking, providing information, education, and support for stepparents, remarried parents, and their children.

692. The Step Family Foundation
333 West End Avenue
New York, New York 10023

    Information clearinghouse on stepfamilies.

693. Widowed Persons Service
1909 K Street, N.W.
Washington, D.C. 20049

    A program of the American Association of Retired Persons that sponsors widow-to-widow self-help support throughout the country. Publishes a booklet, "On Being Alone," and the "Directory of Services for the Widowed in the United States and Canada," updated annually.

AUTHOR (AND EDITOR) INDEX

Aalberts, Monique, 458
Adams, Bert N., 290, 291
Adams, Jane, 292
Adams, Margaret, 1, 293
Adelson, Joseph, 377
Albrecht, Stan L., 294
Alger, William Rouseville, 2, 295
Allan, Graham A., 3, 4, 296, 297
Allen, Christine M.B., 149
Allon, Natalie, 298
Aneshensel, Carol S., 545
Anderson, Jane, 299
Arezzo, Diana, 260
Argyle, Michael, 5, 6, 147, 300
Aries, Philippe, 7, 8
Aristotle, 9, 211
Arling, Greg, 301, 302
Asher, Steve, 10, 303, 514, 538, 606
Ashton, E.T., 304
Augustine, 11

Babchuk, Nicholas, 305, 306, 307, 308, 309, 317, 607
Bachrach, Leona L., 12
Backman, Carl W., 310
Bacon, Sir Francis, 311
Bald, R. C., 13
Baldassare, Mark, 99
Baehr, Consuelo, 14
Baker, Luther G., 312
Ballweg, John A., 15, 306, 307
Balswick, Jack, 313, 314, 315
Barkas, J. L., 16, 17, 18, 19, 20, 21
Barnes, J. A., 22
Barrett, Carol J., 316
Bart, Pauline B., 558
Barzun, Jacques, 286

Basnor, Philip S., 318
Bates, Alan P., 308, 317
Baulch, Norma, 367
Becker, Howard S., 319, 320
Beidelman, Thomas O., 321
Bell, Julian, 322
Bell, Robert R., 23, 323
Belo, Jane, 324
Belmont, David Eugene, 24
Benedict, Ruth, 25
Bensman, Joseph, 26, 325
Berendt, Thomas J., 608
Berger, Peter L., 27, 28, 29, 326
Berkman, L.F., 327
Berkowitz, Bernard, 207
Berkowitz, S.D., 30
Bernard, Jessie, 31
Berne, Eric, 32
Bernikow, Louise, 33, 328, 329
Berscheid, Ellen, 34, 157, 370
Bigelow, Brian J., 330, 331, 332, 333, 610, 639
Black, Hugh, 35
Blankenship, Virginia, 149
Blau, Peter M., 36, 334
Blau, Zena Smith, 37, 38, 335
Block, Joel D., 39, 336, 337
Blum, Alan F., 40, 338
Blum, Lawrence A., 41
Bochner, Arthur, 625
Bohannon, Paul, 339, 340
Boissevain, Jeremy, 42, 43
Bok, Sissela, 44, 45
Bolotin, David, 46
Booth, Alan, 309, 341, 342
Booth, G., 47
Borman, Kathryn M.
Bott, Elizabeth, 48
Brain, Robert, 49
Brennan, Tim, 343
Brenner, Jeffrey, 344

Brenton, Myron, 50
Broderick, Carlfred Bartholomew, 51
Brody, Jane E., 345
Brown, Carol A., 346
Brown, Donald R., 149
Brown, George W., 147
Brown, Helen Gurley, 52
Brown, Irene Q., 347
Brown, Roger
Bry, Adelaid, 53
Buber, Martin, 54, 211
Buehler, John A., 349
Bultena, Gordon L., 364, 534
Burgess, Robert L., 141, 440
Burns, Steven D., 354, 356
Burns, Tom, 348
Burton, Charles Emory, 55
Byrne, Donn, 349

Caldwell, Mayta A., 350
Callenbach, Ernest, 167
Candy, Sandra Gibbs, 351
Cannon, Lynn Weber, 352
Cargan, Leonard, 56
Carnegie, Dale, 57
Carnes, Donald E., 569
Carpentar, Edward, 58
Cary, David MacKenzie, 59
Cash, Thomas F., 353, 354, 355, 356, 357, 612
Cate, Rodney M., 441
Cerreto, Mary, 507
Chaikin, Alan, 76, 375
Challman, Robert C., 348
Chambliss, William Joseph, 60, 359
Chapman, Anthony J., 101, 409
Chasin, Gerald, 61
Chelune, Gordon, 62
Christensen, A., 157
Cicero, 63
Clark, Walter, 466
Clarke, David D., 149
Clutton-Brock, Arthur, 360

Coelho, George V., 361
Cohen, Bernard P., 64
Cohen, Steven Martin, 65
Cohen, Yehudi A., 362
Collins, Glenn, 363
Conner, Karen A., 364
Cook, Karen S., 365
Cooper, John M., 366
Cott, Nancy, 66
Corsaro, William A., 10, 368
Cowgill, Donald O., 367
Cozby, P. C., 369
Crabbe, B. D., 575
Crader, Kelly Wayne, 67
Crotts, Gail, 564

Damon, William, 68
Darley, John M., 370
Dauer, Edward A., 371
Davidson, Laurie, 69, 372
Davidson, Lynne R.
Davidson, Sherwin, 373
Davis, E. Donald, 374
Davis, Murray S., 70
Dawley, Harold H., 71
Day, Barbara Ruth, 72
de Beauvoir, Simone, 73
Degler, Carl N., 74
Denney, Reuel, 229
Denzin, Norman K., 189
Derlega, Valerian, 75, 76, 355, 375, 669
Dickens, Wenda J., 376
Dickson, Sara, 149
Douvan, Elizabeth, 377
Dowling, Colette, 77
Duberman, Lucile, 372
DuBois, Cora, 171, 611
Duck, Steve, 78, 79, 80, 81, 82, 83, 84, 85, 86, 378, 379, 380, 381, 382, 383, 384, 385, 386, 501, 613, 614, 690
Dunphy, Dexter C., 387
Durkheim, Emile, 87, 88

Eckerman, Carol O., 388
Eder, Donna, 389
Edman, Irwin
Edminston, Susan
Edney, Julian J., 390
Edwards, John N., 391, 392
Edwards, Marie, 89
Eggleston, Lynn, 615
Ehrenreich, Barbara, 393
Eichenbaum, Luise, 394
Eisenstadt, S. N., 395
Embree, John F., 90
Emerson, Ralph Waldo, 211, 396
Emerson, Richard M., 365
Epstein, J. L., 92, 616, 617
Epstein, Joseph, 91
Erikson, Erik H., 93, 94
Erwin, P. G., 618
Etzioni, Amitai, 398
Etzkowitz, Henry, 619

Faderman, Lillian, 95
Farrell, Michael, 620, 621
Fasteau, Marc Feigen, 96
Feinberg, Paul, 97
Feldberg, Roslyn, 346
Fellin, Phillip, 399, 400
Feshbach, Norma D., 622
Festinger, Leon, 401
Fine, Gary Alan, 402, 403, 304
Firth, Raymond, 405
Fischer, Claude S., 98, 99, 406, 407, 497, 623, 624
Fischer, Judith L., 408
Fishel, Diane, 298
Fiske, Adele M., 100
Fitzpatrick, Mary Anne, 625, 626
Foot, Hugh C., 101, 409
Fortier, T. L., 102
Fox, Elizabeth M., 346
Frame, Donald M.
Freeman, Valerie, 357
Freud, Anna, 103
Fried, Charles, 410, 411

Friedman, Edward Philip, 104
Fromm, Erich, 105
Fromm-Reichmann, Frieda, 412
Furman, Wyndol, 413, 414, 415, 627

Gaebler, Heather C., 385
Gans, Herbert, 106
Gay, F., 107
Gelven, Michael, 108
Gerson, Ann C., 99, 416, 522
Gerson, Kathleen, 99, 574
Gibran, Kahlil, 109
Giele, Janet Zollinger, 417
Gillen, Barry, 356
Gilmour, Robin, 83, 84, 85
Glaser, Barney, 110
Glazer, Nathan, 229
Glazer-Melbin, Nona, 111
Glick, Paul C., 112
Goethals, George W., 113
Goffman, Erving, 114, 115, 116, 117, 118, 418
Goldberg, Herb, 119
Gonso, Jenni, 421
Goode, William J., 120, 121, 419, 420
Gordon, Laura Kramer, 69
Gordon, Suzanne, 122, 423
Gottman, John, 10, 421
Gouldner, Alvin W., 422
Gouldner, Helen Beem, 123
Gove, Walter R., 424, 439
Granovetter, Mark S., 425
Graziano, William G., 426
Greeley, Andrew M., 124
Green, Elise Hart, 427
Gruenberg, Sidonie, 125
Grundmann, Michael J., 390
Gump, P., 535
Gurdin, J. Barry, 126, 629, 630, 631
Guy, Rebecca F., 352

Hacker, Helen Mayer, 428, 632

Hagoel, Lea, 127
Hall, Mary, 584
Hallinan, Maureen T., 389, 429, 582
Hare, A. Paul, 214
Hart, Nicky, 128
Hartup, Willard W., 415, 430, 431
Harvey, J., 157
Haven, Clayton, 490
Hays, Robert B., 146, 432
Hearn, Janice W., 129
Hendershot, Gerry E., 467
Henderson, Monika, 6, 147, 300
Herrick, Shirley L., 130
Herzberger, Sharon, 646
Hess, Beth B., 131, 259, 433, 434
Hess, Elaine, 342
Hess, Thomas G., 149
Hill, Charles T., 435
Hinde, Robert A., 132
Hoffman, Gerhard, 133
Homans, George Caspar, 134, 135, 436
Hoopes, Margaret H., 437
Hoover, Eleanor, 89
Horn, Jack C., 438
Howard, Jane, 136
Howe, M. A. De Wolfe, 137
Howell, Mary C., 138
Hughes, Michael, 439
Hunt, Bernice, 140
Hunt, Morton, 139, 140
Huston, Ted, 141, 157, 440, 441, 442, 443
Hutter, Horst, 142, 631
Hymel, Shelley, 303
Hymer, Sharon, 633

Indvik, Julie, 626, 634
Institute for Social Research, 444, 445
Irish, Donald P., 447
Izard, Carroll E., 448

Jacklin, Carol Nagy, 449
Jackson, Jacquelyne Johnson, 450
Jackson, Robert Max, 99, 451
Jacobson, David, 452
Jacoby, Susan, 453, 454
James, Muriel, 143
Jecker, Jon, 455
Johnson, D. W., 144
Johnson, F. P., 144
Johnson, Joyce S., 520
Johnson, Michael P., 456, 457, 636
de Jon-Gierveld, Jenny, 458, 637
Jones, Lynne McCallister, 99
Jones, Stella B., 459
Jourard, Sidney M., 145, 460
Journal of Social and Personal Relationships, 146, 147, 148, 149, 150

Kadushin, Charles, 151, 461, 462, 463, 641
Kant, Immanuel, 152
Kant, Rosabeth Moss, 153
Karweit, Nancy Lynne, 92, 154
Kaufman, Debra Renee, 155, 464
Kazdin, Alan
Kehr, Jo Anne, 357
Kelley, Eleanor Ann, 156
Kelley, H. H., 157
Kellner, Hansfried, 28, 326
Kennedy, Eugene, 158
Kille, Mary F., 211
Klemesrud, Judy, 465
Klos, Dennis S., 113
Knapp, Mark L., 159
Knat, Steven M., 149
Knupfer, Genevieve, 466
Kobrin, Francis E., 467
Kochen, Manfred, 531
Kohen, Janet, 346
Komarovsky, Mirra, 160

Kon, Igor S., 469
Kornblum, William, 161
Krain, Mark, 469
Krantzler, Mel, 162
Krech, Hilda Sidney, 125
Kurth, Suzanne B., 189

L'Abate, Luciano, 470
La Gaipa, John J., 332, 471, 472, 473, 474, 501, 638, 639
Lahey, Benjamin
Landberg, Michelle, 640
Landy, David, 455
Lang, Olga, 164
La Rochefoucauld, Francois de, 163
Larson, Reed W., 475
Lasch, Christopher, 165, 166
Lazarsfeld, Paul F., 476
Leavitt, Shelley, 260
Leefeldt, Christine, 167
Leff, Arthur Allen, 371
Lepp, Ignace, 168
Leslie, Leigh, 457
Lever, Janet, 477, 478
Levinger, George, 157, 442, 480, 481
Levinson, Daniel J., 169
Levi-Strauss, Claude, 479
Levy, Sheldon G., 351
Lewin, Kurt, 482
Lewis, Michael, 170
Lewis, Robert A., 483
Leyton, Elliot, 171
Libby, Roger W., 484
Liebow, Elliot, 172
Lilienfeld, Robert, 26, 325
Lindsey, Karen, 173
Lipnack, Jessica, 174
Litwak, Eugene, 399, 400, 486
Lively, Penelope, 175
Loomis, Charles P.
Lopata, Helena Znaniecka, 176, 177, 178, 487, 488
Losenkov, Vladimir, 468

Losoff, Michael, 146, 496
Lovenheim, Barbara
Lowenthal, Marjorie Fisk, 489, 490
Luckmann, Thomas, 29
Lynch, James J., 179
Lynd, Helen Merrell, 180
Lynd, Robert S., 180

Maas, Henry S., 491
Maccoby, Eleanor E., 449
MacDonald, Marcia G., 507
Machlowitz, Marilyn, 181
Mahan, Linda, 564
Maines, David, 178
Malinowski, Bronislaw, 182
Mangione, Peter, 646
Martin, Dawson, 492
Marty, Martin E., 183
Maslow, Abraham H., 184
Masselo, Robert, 493
Masterson, George, 185
Mauss, Marcel, 186
May, Rollo, 187
Mayer, John, 494
McAdams, Dan P., 146, 496
McCaffrey, Erika, 642
McCall, George J., 188, 189, 498
McCall, Michael M., 189
McCallister, Lynne, 497
McClintock, E., , 157
McGinnis, Alan Loy, 190
McHugh, Peter, 40, 338
McPherson, Miller
Mead, Margaret, 25, 191, 192, 193, 495
Meilaender, Gilbert C., 194
Melko, Matthew, 56
Mercer, Marilyn, 500
Merrill, Susan Lee, 195
Merton, Robert K., 476
Mettetal, Gwendolyn, 196, 643
Michaelis, David, 197
Michaels, Leonard, 198

Miell, Dorothy, 385, 501, 613
Miles, Josephine, 311
Milgram, Stanley, 502
Miller, Arthur A., 503
Miller, Charles H., 199
Miller, Gerald R., 644
Miller, Stuart, 200
Mills, Laurens Joseph, 201
Mitchell, James Clyde, 43, 202
Montaigne, 504
Moustakis, Clark, 203
Mueller, Edward, 101, 344, 505, 506
Murstein, Bernard I., 204, 507, 508
Musser, Lynn Mather, 426

Naegele, Kaspar D., 509
Narus, Leonard J., Jr., 408
Nelson, Joel I., 510
Nemy, Enid, 511
Neugarten, Bernice L., 512
Neuwirth, Gertrud R., 205
Newcomb, Theodore M., 206, 513
Newman, Mildred, 207
Nietzsche, Friedrich, 208, 209
Nisbet, Robert A., 210
Noonan, John Ford, 645
Norton, Arthur J., 112
Norton, David L., 211

Oakes, Thomas Warren, 212
O'Connell, Lenahan, 148
O'Connor, Pat, 147
Oden, Sherri Lee, 213, 514, 646
Oliker, Stacey J., 624
Olmsted, Michael S., 214
Orbach, Susie, 394
O'Shea, Robert Michael, 216
Oskamp, Stuart, 515
Osofsky, Joy D., 215

Packard, Ted, 373
Packard, Vance, 516

Paine, Robert, 517
Parks, Malcolm R., 644
Parlee, Mary Brown, 518
Parsons, Talcott, 217, 218, 519
Paykel, Eugene S., 591
Pearlin, Leonard I., 520, 521
Peplau, Letitia Anne, 157, 219, 350, 435, 523, 550, 647
Perlman, Daniel, 86, 219, 376, 416, 515, 522, 523, 614, 647
Petersen, Elwnoe Langston, 220
Peterson, D.,157
Petrowsky, Marc, 524
Philips, Gerald M., 221
Phillips, Derek L., 525
Pines, Maya, 526
Pitt-Rivers, Julian, 527, 528
Plath, David W., 529
Plato, 211, 222, 223
Pleck, Joseph, 224, 530
Plutarch, 225
Polyson, James, 357
Pool, Ithiel de Sola, 531
Population Reference Bureau, Inc., 532
Potashin, Reva, 533
Potter, Hannah C., 555
Potter, Ralph B., 648, 649
Powers, Edward A., 364, 534
Press, Irwin
Price, Richard, 226
<u>Psychology Today</u> editors, 518

Rahe, Donald F., 415
Ramsoy, Odd, 446
Rasmussen, Brian, 421
Redl, F., 535
Reina, Ruben E., 536
Reisman, John M., 227, 537
Renshaw, Peter D., 538
Reohr, J., 228
Rich, Adrienne
Richardson, H. M., 539
Riesman, David, 229

Risoli, Toni, 650, 651
Roberts, John M., 540
Robertson, Joan F., 600
Robins, Elliot, 443
Rodin, M. J., 541
Rollin, Betty, 542
Rollins, Judy, 543
Rolon, Michael E., 230
Room, Robin, 466
Rooney, James Francis, 231
Rose, Arnold M., 544
Rose, Suzanne M., 148
Rosen, Bernard C., 545
Rosenberg, S., 621
Rosenblatt, Roger, 546
Rosenblum, Leonard A., 170
Rosow, Irving, 232, 547
Rossi, Alice S.
Rossi, Peter H., 233
Roth, Guenther
Rousseau, Jean Jacques, 286
Rubin, Lillian Breslow, 234, 235
Rubin, Zick, 236, 237, 435, 548, 549, 550, 551, 652
Ryan, John, 552
Rysman, Alexander Romm, 238

Safilios-Rothschild, Constantina, 553
Salamon, Sonya, 554
Sants, Harriet, 148, 386
Saunders, Janice M., 392
Sarma, Jyotirmoyee, 238
Sawyer, Jack, 224
Savary, Louis M., 143
Schofield, Janet Ward, 668
Schofield, William, 240
Schonberg, William B., 555
Schooler, Carmi, 521
Schopenhauer, 211, 241
Schur, E. M., 242
Schwartz, Barry, 556
Sebald, Hans, 243
Secord, Paul F., 310

Seiden, Anne M., 557, 558
Selden, Elizabeth S., 244
Selman, Anne P., 559
Selman, Robert L., 245, 559
Seneca, Gail, 246
Shain, Merle, 247, 248
Sharabany, R., 560
Sheehy, Gail, 249
Shenker, Stephen, 551
Shils, Edward A., 218
Shulman, Norman, 561
Shuval, Judith T., 250
Simmel, Georg, 251, 252, 562, 563
Simmons, J. L., 188, 498
Simon, Rita James, 564
Sklar, Kathryn Kish, 655
Slater, Philip E., 253
Smiley, Jane, 254
Smith, J. R., 101, 409
Smith, Johnathan, 577
Smith, M. Estellie, 563
Smith-Lovin, L., 499
Smith-Rosenberg, Carroll, 565, 656
Smucker, Orden C., 255
Snyder, Howard N., 668
Sojourner, 566
Somers, Ann R., 567
Srole, Leo, 256
Sparks, James Allen, 257
Spinner, Barry, 522
Spitz, Leah T., 508
Spock, Benjamin, 568
Stamps, Jeffrey, 174
Starr, Joyce R., 569
Stein, Harry, 570, 571
Stein, Peter J., 258, 259, 572, 619, 659, 660
Stock, St. George, 397
Stocking, S. Holly, 260
Stone, Gregory P., 573
Stoodley, Bartlett H.
Stouffer, Samuel A., 218
Straus, A.L., 110

Strong, Leslie Dale, 261
Stueve, C. Ann, 99, 574
Sullivan, Harry Stack, 262
Surra, Catherine, 661
Sutcliffe, J. P., 575
Suttles, Gerald D., 189
Sutton-Smith, Brian, 535
Syme, Leonard, 327
Szelenyi, Ivan, 486

Taylor, Jeremy, 263
Tennov, Dorothy, 264
Tesich, Steve, 576
Tesser, Abraham, 577
Theroux, Paul
Thompson, Linda, 578
Thoreau, Henry David, 265
Tiger, Lionel, 266
Toby, Jackson, 218
Todd, Janet M., 267
Tognoli, Jerome, 579
Tomeh, Aida K., 580
Tonnies, Ferdinand, 268
Toomey, D. M., 581
Troll, Lillian E., 351
Troyat, Henri, 269
Tschann, Jeanne M., 270
Tuma, N. B.
Turner, R. Jay, 583

Udry, Richard, 584
U.S. Department of Commerce, 664, 665, 666
Useem, Michael, 271
Useem, Ruth, 320

Vaillant, George E., 272
Van Gennep, Arnold, 273
Vandell, Deborah Lowe, 101
Vaughan, Diane, 585
Verbrugge, Lois Marie, 274, 586, 587, 588

Walker, Alexis J., 578
Wallach, Anne Tolstoi, 275

Walster, Elaine, 34, 276
Walster, G. William, 276
Weber, Max, 277, 278
Weinberg, S. Kirson, 589
Weinraub, Bernard
Weiss, Robert S., 259, 279, 280, 590
Weissman, Myrna M., 591
Wellman, Barry, 30
Whatley, Judith L., 388
Wheeler, Valerie A., 606, 646, 667
Whitley, Bernard E., 668
Whyte, William Foote, 281, 282
Williams, James Howard, 283, 592
Williams, Robin M., 593
Wilmot, William W., 284
Wilmott, Peter, 287
Winslow, C. N., 594
Winstead, B., 75
Wirth, Louis, 595
Wittich, Claus
Wolf, Eric R., 596
Wolfe, Linda, 597
Wolff, Kurt H.
Wolfenstein, Martha, 193
Women's Action Alliance, Inc.
Wong, Herbert, 599
Wong, Paul T. P., 669
Wood, Julia T., 221
Wood, Margaret M., 285
Woods, Ralph L., 286
Woods, Vivian, 600
Wright, Paul H., 146, 601, 602, 603

Yamokoshi, T., 537
Young, Michael, 287

Zaslow, Martha, 670
Zewe, Martin Donald, 288
Zimbardo, Philip G., 289

SUBJECT INDEX

acquaintanceship, 17, 18, 80, 114, 206, 349, 425, 509, 531, 612, 627
adolescence and friendship, 18, 67, 84, 85, 103, 113, 133, 161, 243, 262, 332, 343, 376, 377, 380, 387, 468, 472, 475, 557, 604, 617, 628, 640, 654
altruism, 41
Aristotle, 9, 17, 63, 211, 311, 318, 366, 504, 508
attraction, 34, 87, 310, 355, 357, 385, 442, 513, 612

Bacon, Sir Francis, 33, 311
beauty, 353, 354, 355, 356
bibliographies on friendship, 4, 17, 23, 361, 607, 611, 642, 648, 649, 650, 651
birth order, 580
blood brotherhood, 49, 321, 395, 528
Buber, Martin, 54, 211

childhood, 7, 68, 93
    See also adolescence, infancy, toddlers
children's friendships, 18, 78, 84, 125, 146, 213, 260, 303, 330, 331, 332, 333, 344, 358, 363, 368, 376, 385, 388, 389, 402, 409, 413, 414, 415, 421, 427, 429, 430, 431, 449, 471, 477, 491, 496, 506, 514, 533, 538, 559, 568, 573, 608, 618, 639, 646
China, 164, 361
Cicero, 17, 63, 396, 504
cities See urban life
class variations in friendship, 3, 4, 15, 48, 161, 296, 564, 581, 631
cliques, 93, 104, 510
commitment, 319, 365, 456, 636
communication, 159, 190, 196, 221, 284, 385, 416, 506, 537, 599, 643, 644
conflict, 82, 167, 251, 427, 667
courtship, 23, 70, 264, 298, 457, 469, 661
cross-sex friendships See opposite-sex friendships
cultural variations in friendship, 25, 49, 65, 90, 193, 300, 361, 362, 395, 486, 495, 509, 528

death, 8, 680, 693 See also widowhood
dependency, 70, 77, 337, 545
differentiated friendships, 252
divorce, 39, 91, 112, 120, 128, 139, 140, 162, 280, 294,
    339, 340, 346, 392, 480, 503, 585, 615
    See also separation
dyad, 17, 188, 252, 284, 320, 578

elderly friendships, 37, 84, 104, 232, 301, 302, 335, 342,
    364, 376, 434, 489, 490, 522, 524, 534, 547, 548, 555,
    600 See also widowhood

embarrassment, 418
Emerson, Ralph Waldo, 33, 211, 396
enemies, 40, 348
exchange theory See social exchange
expectations, 36, 165, 330, 332, 639, 640

family See kinship
female friendships, 1, 2, 17, 18, 23, 33, 66, 71, 74, 123,
    167, 196, 221, 275, 292, 323, 329, 350, 351, 355, 372,
    393, 408, 423, 428, 450, 454, 465, 494, 500, 511, 558,
    565, 566, 589, 598, 632, 645, 655, 656
friendly kin relations, 17
friendship:
    after forty, 257 See also elderly friendships
    at college, 17, 185, 255, 350, 539
    at work, 49, 55, 119, 123, 131, 155, 161, 282, 423,
        464, 500, 511, 542, 587, 629, 634
    casual, 373
    children's, 18, 84, 125, 146, 213, 260, 303, 330, 331,
        332, 333, 344, 358, 363, 368, 376, 385, 388, 389,
        402, 409, 413, 414, 415, 421, 427, 429, 430, 431,
        449, 471, 477, 491, 496, 506, 514, 533, 538, 559,
        568, 573, 608, 618, 639, 646
    class variations, 3, 4, 15, 48, 161, 235, 296, 564,
        581, 631
    clergy, 178
    cross-sex See opposite-sex
    definition, 4, 17, 18, 189, 373, 407, 509, 517, 518,
        652
    differentiated, 252
    dissolution, 17, 81, 148, 236, 383, 384, 426, 456,
        608, 638, 644

elderly, 37, 84, 104, 232, 301, 302, 335, 342, 364, 376, 434, 489, 490, 522, 524, 534, 547, 548, 555, 600 See also widowhood
ethics of, 9, 11, 648, 649
famous, 33, 197, 199, 269
female, 1, 2, 17, 33, 66, 71, 74, 123, 167, 196, 221, 275, 292, 323, 329, 350, 351, 355, 372, 393, 408, 423, 428, 450, 454, 465, 494, 500, 511, 558, 565, 566, 589, 598, 632, 645, 655, 656
fictional accounts, 13, 14, 17, 24, 175, 198, 226, 254, 275, 645
health aspects, 18, 82, 179, 304, 327, 345, 439, 467, 490, 567, 583, 663
history of, 4, 178, 347, 487, 546, 565
homosexual, 95
in infancy, 101, 170, 215, 236, 388, 449
initiation, 17, 57, 79, 126, 129, 426, 476, 514, 646
interracial, 133, 429, 582, 668
Israeli kibbutz, 178, 361, 670
maintenance, 17, 51, 53, 129, 146, 236, 337, 432, 476
male, 169, 172, 200, 221, 224, 266, 323, 336, 350, 355, 372, 408, 451, 483, 530, 570, 571, 574, 576, 579, 589, 621, 632, 659
manager's wives, 153
married couples, 18, 39, 160, 167, 246, 280, 305, 308, 328, 352, 376, 507, 584
married women, 247, 248
military, 178
opposite-sex, 1, 17, 18, 39, 342, 408, 428, 493, 566, 576, 632
over life cycle, 18, 84, 178, 259, 270, 376, 433, 561, 574, 616, 621, 624
romantic, 95
rules of, 9, 63, 109, 147, 189, 300
same-sex See female friendships or male friendships
selection, 51, 59, 60, 61, 64, 72, 359, 380, 382, 451, 513, 588
surveys, 39, 518
toddlers, 170, 178, 236, 344, 363, 427, 670

gender differences in friendship, 270, 323, 342, 350, 372, 377, 389, 394, 433, 449, 464, 477, 478, 534, 560, 625, 632
gift-giving, 186, 556
Goffman, Erving, 36, 114, 115, 116, 117, 118, 418

gossip, 153, 196
Greek philosophers, 4, 9, 24, 46, 58, 361, 397, 648, 649
guilt, 108

happiness, 56, 57, 525, 552
housewives, 176, 283, 592

intimacy, 26, 70, 76, 234, 325, 351, 490, 553, 599, 637
intimacy problems in men, 111, 119, 313, 314, 315, 394,
    470, 483, 530

Japan, 90, 300, 361, 529, 554

kinship, 3, 4, 48, 121, 136, 166, 287, 290, 306, 307, 450,
    457, 467, 475, 486, 510, 519, 554, 561, 565, 587, 596,
    600, 664

lawyer as friend, 371, 410, 411, 492
leisure time, 56, 180, 367
literary view of friendship, 13, 33, 58, 175, 201, 267, 295
Little League, 402, 404
living together, 112, 204
loneliness, 49, 56, 71, 85, 86, 122, 179, 203, 219, 253,
    279, 328, 343, 345, 412, 416, 488, 522, 523, 543, 549,
    606, 637, 647
love, 49, 70, 105, 187, 211, 237, 252, 264, 276, 396, 419,
    562 See also courtship
lying, 44
Lysis, 46, 222, 318

male friendships, 23, 169, 172, 200, 221, 224, 266, 272,
    323, 336, 350, 355, 372, 408, 451, 483, 530, 570, 571,
    574, 576, 579, 589, 621, 632, 659
marriage, 27, 31, 65,112, 145, 234, 280, 292, 326, 424,
    444, 465, 518, 520, 552, 581, 586, 661 See also
    friendship, married couples, married women
mental health, 256, 439, 445, 466, 467, 489, 520, 583, 586,
    663 See also friendship, health aspects of
mental illness See mental health
Middletown (USA), 180
mobility, 122, 131, 233, 399, 400, 459, 485, 591
motivation, 184, 338, 603

narcissism, 165, 526, 633
neighbors, 301, 399, 400, 451, 486, 547, 561, 574, 587

networks, 17, 22, 42, 43, 48, 86, 98, 136, 151, 154, 172, 174, 202, 327, 365, 457, 461, 462, 463, 497, 524, 531, 581, 584, 620, 641, 661

opposite-sex friendships, 1, 17, 18, 39, 342, 408, 428, 493, 566, 576, 632

parenting, 574, 624, 688, 691, 692
Parsons, Talcott, 36, 217, 218, 361, 519
patterns of friendship, 17, 362, 536
    dissolution, 17, 81, 148, 236, 383, 384, 426, 456, 608, 638, 644
    initiation, 17, 57, 79, 126, 129, 426, 476, 514, 646
    maintenance, 17, 51, 53, 129, 146, 236, 337, 432, 476
    selection, 51, 59, 60, 61, 64, 72, 359, 380, 382, 451, 513, 588
peer relations See friendship
Plato, 46, 211, 222, 223, 318
power, 36, 57, 351, 365
professional associations, 671, 672, 673, 674, 675, 676, 677, 679, 683, 685, 687, 690
proximity, 17, 18, 451, 476, 551, 593
psychotherapy, 145, 151, 240, 461, 537
puberty, 25 See also adolescence

reciprocity, 36, 54, 149, 228, 422, 479, 667 See also social exchange
reference groups, 231
retirement, 37, 232
role strain, 218, 420
romantic friendships, 95, 566
rural friendships, 438, 575 See also cultural variations

same-sex friendships See female friendships, male friendships
school friendships, 154, 178, 216, 389, 477, 478, 496, 509, 582, 667, 668 See also adolescent friendships, children's friendships, friendship at college
Schopenhauer, Arthur, 211, 648
secrets, 45, 562
self-concept, 103, 105, 602
self-disclosure, 45, 145, 190, 196, 372, 375, 428, 460, 501, 551, 599, 612, 643, 669
self-help groups, 19, 280, 678, 680, 681, 686, 688, 691, 692, 693

separation, 280, 435, 590 See also divorce
sex roles, 69, 408, 417, 609 See also gender differences
    in friendship
shyness, 289
siblings, 297, 447 See also kinship, friendly kin
    relations
sick role behavior, 212
Simmel, Georg, 36, 251, 252, 361, 372, 562, 563
singleness and friendship, 1, 17, 18, 20, 89, 112, 258,
    298, 299, 312, 437, 444, 458, 466, 484, 569, 572, 660
small group behavior, 214, 390, 398, 401
social control, 28, 517
social exchange, 36, 134, 135, 141, 148, 230, 365, 391,
    436, 440, 441, 455, 507
social integration, 334, 439
social network See networks
socialization, 69, 232, 431, 434
status change, 37, 38, 110, 128, 273
stigma, 118, 412
strangers, 40, 70, 285
suburban friendships, 128, 593, 645
suicide, 88, 681

Taylor, Jeremy, 33
therapy See psychotherapy
time management, 16
transactional analysis, 32
triad, 17, 252 See also Simmel

urban friendships, 17, 48, 98, 99, 106, 127, 202, 281, 406,
    438, 461, 575, 592, 597
urban life, 563, 595

Weber, Max, 36, 277, 278, 361
widowhood, 18, 37, 177, 178, 291, 301, 302, 316, 605, 693
    See also elderly friendships
workaholics, 181

Author's Biography

J.L. Barkas has a Ph.D. in sociology and is an Assistant Professor in the Department of Behavioral Sciences at New York Institute of Technology. Dr. Barkas' published books include: Creative Time Management (Prentice-Hall, 1984), How to Write Like a Professional (Prentice-Hall/Arco, 1984), Single in America (Atheneum, 1980), The Help Book (Scribner's, 1979), Victims (Scribner's, 1978), and The Vegetable Passion (Scribner's, 1975), as well as Japanese, Dutch, and British editions of several titles. Her doctoral dissertation was on the friendship patterns of urban single women, and she is the author of a booklet, "Friendship Throughout Life," published in 1983 by the Public Affairs Committee. Her magazine, newspaper, and journal credits include: The New York Times, Harper's, Journal of Current Social Issues, Federal Probation, Glamour, Redbook, The Los Angeles Times, McCall's, Modern Bride, Opera News, The New Leader, Crime and Delinquency Literature, Family Circle, Seventeen, Chicago Tribune, and others. Barkas is a member of numerous professional associations including American Sociological Association, Clinical Sociology Association, and the National Organization of Victim Assistance.